Black Gold

Black Gold
The Story of Oil in Our Lives

Albert Marrin

Alfred A. Knopf
New York

THIS IS A BORZOI BOOK PUBLISHED BY ALFRED A. KNOPF

Text copyright © 2012 by Albert Marrin
Cover art copyright © 2012 by Alfred A. Knopf
Cover Photoshop art by Ericka O'Rourke
Cover photograph of oil copyright © by Shutterstock
Cover photograph of Earth courtesy of NASA

For image credits, please see page 169.

Visit us on the Web! randomhouse.com/teens

Educators and librarians, for a variety of teaching tools, visit us at RHTeachersLibrarians.com

The Library of Congress has cataloged the hardcover edition of this work as follows:
Marrin, Albert.
Black gold : the story of oil in our lives / Albert Marrin. — 1st ed.
p. cm.
Includes bibliographical references, glossary, and index.
ISBN 978-0-375-86673-9 (trade) — ISBN 978-0-375-96673-6 (lib. bdg.) —
ISBN 978-0-375-89686-6 (ebook)
1. Petroleum—United States—History. I. Title.
TN872.A5M39 2012
553.2'8—dc23
2011013175

ISBN 978-0-375-85968-7 (tr. pbk.)

Printed in the United States of America

January 2013

10 9 8 7 6 5 4 3 2 1

First Trade Paperback Edition

For today's young people, who will be confronted by the problem of black gold tomorrow.

There is nothing new in the world except the history you do not know.

—President Harry S. Truman

CONTENTS

Prologue

How Daddy Nearly Blew Himself Up

I've had this book in me for most of my life. In 1943, when I was seven years old, we lived in New York City. World War II was raging, and my father headed an important construction project in another state. Usually, if we were lucky, he drove home on weekends. Though gasoline was rationed, and most people could only buy a few gallons a week, it was never a problem for Dad. He had a government "priority," which meant that his work allowed him to get as much as he needed.

One night, he did not come at the time we expected. We were worried, until we heard the key turning in the lock. Dad was dirty, bruised, and shaken. Instead of the usual suitcase, he carried a clock, torn from the dashboard of the family car, with black wires dangling from it. A souvenir, he said, from "the Old Lady," as he called our beloved car. She had skidded on an icy road, turned over, and slid down an embankment, landing on her roof. Luckily, the highway patrol arrived and pried him from the wreck. He had just enough time, before the explosion, to pull out the clock.

"Explosion?" my mother asked, stunned. "Why an explosion?"

Well, he explained, he had (unwisely) filled the backseat with cans of gasoline. He was taking it to another job in New York, "just in case."

"Why?" Mother asked, hardly believing her ears.

"Don't you know," he said, "that gas is precious these days? This stuff runs the world."

I have never forgotten those words. For nothing has changed since that long-ago night. Today, as then, oil and its chief by-product, gasoline, still run the world. However, nothing lasts forever. The amount of oil is limited. As it becomes harder to find and more expensive to get out of the ground, it will grow yet more precious. Controlling its supply, and finding substitutes for it, will shape much of the social, political, and military history of the twenty-first century. That is what this book is about.

I
A FREAK OF GEOLOGY

*The stuff we pump into our gas tanks is a freak of
geology, the product of a series of lucky breaks
over millions of years.*

—Tim Appenzeller
Science Editor, National Geographic

Of Earth and Living Beings

Oil is not pretty. When it is taken from beneath the earth's surface, it is
called crude oil, or crude for short. Although crude can be green, red,
straw-colored, or chocolate brown, it is usually black. Because it is so
valuable, in the late 1800s people in the industry nicknamed it "black
gold." Since then, it has made fortunes for the lucky few and provided
jobs for millions of ordinary folks.

   Thick and slippery, crude oil has an evil smell, giving off vapors
that make eyes watery and throats sore. Yet without it, life as we live it
today would be impossible. Oil fuels the engines that move us and our
goods from place to place. It heats our homes and powers the machines
that make the everyday things we take for granted. Thousands of products, from drinking straws to plastic shopping bags, from plant fertilizer
to computers and medical equipment, begin as crude oil. So do most

school backpacks, knee guards—even the yellow "rubber" duck floating in your bathtub. Modern weapons such as tanks, aircraft, and ships are so much metallic junk without oil products to make them run.

Oil influences every aspect of modern life. It has helped shape the history, society, politics, and economy of every nation on Earth. Nations have fought wars for black gold and, sadly, probably will do so in the future. Yet few who rely on this vital substance know much about it. What, exactly, is oil? How was it formed? When? Where?

To understand oil, we must begin with a key rule of science: change alone is changeless. This may sound odd, but it is true. Nothing stays the same forever. Change governs everything in the universe, from distant galaxies, stars, and planets to tiny bacteria and giant whales—and us humans, too. Many changes in nature, such as the formation of mountains, happen too slowly for us to notice, unfolding over many lifetimes, even millions of years. When we do see rapid and sudden changes, they are usually bad for us. For example, the people of the Italian city of Pompeii had lived for generations in the shadow of Mount Vesuvius, a dormant, or "sleeping," volcano. In the year AD 79, the sleeper awoke with an outburst of flame and fury. Within hours, it sent clouds of hot ash and gas to choke over 20,000 people, nearly all of Pompeii's residents.

Mountain ranges and volcanoes are features of the geology of the planet Earth. Geology is the science that studies the structure and history of the earth as recorded in the rocks. If you could slice deep into the earth, you would find that it is arranged in layers. Geologists—earth scientists—believe that the topmost layer of rock, or crust, is between four and forty miles thick. Earth's crust is like an eggshell broken into ten enormous slabs and numerous smaller ones. These slabs, called plates, float on a layer of partially molten rock called the mantle—that is, the layer of rock between Earth's crust and core.

Every continent and ocean floor rests atop one or more plates. Driven by heat currents from Earth's core, plates are always in motion, always changing position. Although the plates move slowly, just a few inches a year, their movements have shaped Earth's crust—and

2

still do. Moving plates push against, slide past, and grind under one another. When two plates scrunch together, they trigger earthquakes that create volcanoes and mountain ranges such as the Rockies, Andes, and Himalayas.

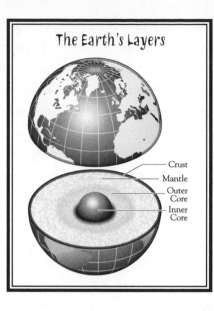

The Earth's Layers

Crust
Mantle
Outer Core
Inner Core

Yet not even a mountain range can resist the force of flowing water. Water is invincible. Given enough time, it will erode—wear away—the hardest rocks. Rushing rivers break off bits of rock. Carried downstream, these bits bounce along a river's bottom, or bed, further shattering into coarse gravel or grains of fine sand.

Inevitably, rivers lose power as they run off from a continent and enter an ocean. In doing so, they drop the materials they carried, called sediment, into the coastal waters. Tides and currents move the sediment into deeper waters, far from shore. Settling on the ocean floor, it slowly builds up in layers that may become miles thick. As the lower, older sediment layers get buried deeper, the weight of the upper, younger layers compresses and hardens them, turning them to stone. These are the layers we see along the walls of deep cuts in Earth's surface, such as the walls of the Grand Canyon of the Colorado River. The mighty Colorado carved its canyon over millions of years, as it still does today.

Life began in the oceans, thanks to the sun. Nearly ninety-three million miles from Earth, the sun, like other stars, is a glowing ball of hot gases. Most of the sun's energy, in the form of light, is lost in deep space. However, a tiny fraction reaches Earth, where it drives the weather by heating the atmosphere and oceans, fueling life.

Ancient peoples worshipped the sun. For them, sunlight symbolized life, while darkness symbolized death—eternal night. Although the ancients could not explain why, modern science has shown how sunlight sustains life on Earth. From about 3.8 to 2.5 billion years ago, the first plants and animals developed in the oceans. Over millions of years, some of these changed, or evolved, in ways that allowed them to move onto the land. Every land plant and animal alive today has ancestors that once emerged from the oceans.

Like their modern kin, the earliest life-forms were what scientists call self-feeders. These are green plants, which trap solar energy through photosynthesis—that is, the process of turning sunlight into chemical energy. Energy is the power to do work or to act. Green plants store chemical energy and use it to live, especially to turn it into food for themselves. Thus, they are self-feeders.

4

Animals are other-feeders, or consumers. No animal can make its own food. To live, some animals must feed on plants, absorbing the chemical energy stored in them. Other animals, however, get their energy in another way. Carnivores, or flesh eaters, eat the plant eaters and other flesh eaters, too.

A fossil of a carboniferous leaf, *Alethopteris serii*, unearthed in Somerset, England.

Most living beings vanish after they die. Microscopic bacteria nearly always consume the remains of the dead, leaving no trace. We call this decay. Yet, occasionally, some naturally preserved remains survive. These remains of ancient life-forms are fossils, from the Latin word *fossilis*, for "dug up." Generally, only the hard parts survive as fossils. These include bones, teeth, shells, and the woody parts of plants that become petrified, or turned to stone, by absorbing minerals from the earth. Other fossils are not the actual remains of an animal or plant at all, but imprints of them left in mud that hardened before decay set in. Studying fossils can help us understand what Earth was like in the distant past and how life-forms changed over time. But most of us have no use for such fossils in our daily lives.

Fossil Fuels

Fossil fuels *are* useful. A fuel is any material that stores energy. Like ordinary fossils, fossil fuels are the remains of plant life from the distant past. Yet they are nothing like the plant fossils we see in museums. Instead of resembling the plants they once were, fossil fuels have a different appearance because chemical changes have taken place. Nevertheless, fossil fuels store the chemical energy the original plants took from sunlight ages ago. Burning fossil fuels releases their captured energy so that we can put it to work for us.

5

Fossil fuels were formed when ancient plants died and were buried under layers of sediment deposited by water. There are three kinds of fossil fuels: coal, oil, and natural gas. Scientists use a special term for such fuels: hydrocarbons. This is because each contains various amounts of hydrogen and carbon, the chemical building blocks of all life on Earth. Hydrocarbons supply nearly all the energy that powers today's world.

Coal deserves its nickname, "buried sunshine." It is the most abundant fossil fuel and the one that humans have used the longest. Most coal formed during the Carboniferous Period, the time in Earth's history from about 360 million to 285 million years ago; *carboniferous* is Latin for "coal-bearing." The world's climate then was warmer and moister than it is today, even at the North and South Poles. Swamps covered vast areas of the continents. Towering trees, ferns, and other leafy plants grew in the swamps. Giant dragonflies, often with wingspans two feet across, darted through the air, chasing other giant insects. The first reptiles, ancestors of the dinosaurs, roamed the land.

Coal began to form when the remains of dead plants sank to the bottom of the swamps they grew in. Sediment deposited by streams and rivers covered the remains. Centuries passed as generation upon generation of plants died and were buried under layers of mud and sand. New layers constantly formed. And as they did, the weight of the younger layers bore down on the older layers beneath them. Gradually, increasing pressure squeezed out the water, so the remains of the plants, all scrunched together, hardened and lost their original shape. Or most of them did, for miners sometimes find leaf impressions made in coal millions of years ago. Pressure and hardening drove out the hydrogen gas and other ingredients like sulfur, leaving black carbon: coal.

Yet not all coal is equal. Coal's hardness depends on the amount of pressure and time it took to form. The more carbon it contains, the more energy it will release in the form of heat.

Coal begins as peat (60 percent carbon), a tangled, soggy mass of decaying roots, branches, stems, and leaves. Although used for fuel, especially in Ireland, where it is abundant, peat gives off little heat and much smoke. Next comes lignite, or brown coal (73 percent carbon), a harder substance that burns hotter than peat, but not much. Power plants burn lignite mainly to generate electricity and because it is cheap. Bituminous, or soft, coal (85 percent carbon) is black in color and harder than lignite; it gives enough heat for cooking and warming homes. Anthracite, the hardest coal of all (over 90 percent carbon), is buried deepest and longest. Because it burns hottest, anthracite is ideal for smelting—that is, heating certain types of rocks, called ores, to melt out the metal they contain. We get tin, copper, and iron this way.

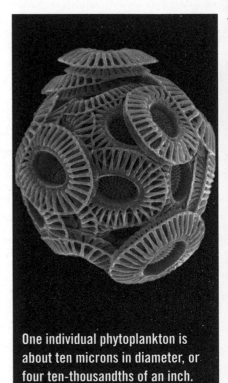

Oil and natural gas are formed differently from coal. Both are the remains of lifeforms called phytoplankton that lived in the oceans between 10

One individual phytoplankton is about ten microns in diameter, or four ten-thousandths of an inch.

million and 260 million years ago, in the time of the dinosaurs. "Phytoplankton" comes from the Greek words *phyton* (for "plant") and *planktos* (for "wanderer" or "drifter"). Too small to move on their own, phytoplankton float near the surface, in the sunlit zone of the ocean, to carry on photosynthesis. While there are hundreds of species of plankton, most are plants no larger than a grain of sand or a pinhead. Diatoms, perhaps the most common type, are single-celled plants covered by two shells that look glossy. Scientists have named about 20,000 species of diatoms. Given the right conditions, a single diatom can produce 100 million offspring each month. Like other plants, phytoplankton chemically store sunlight as energy to make food.

Phytoplankton have probably always been the oceans' most abundant life-form. Thanks to them, life there is an elaborate web, with each strand depending on the others for survival. Immense clouds of phytoplankton, each numbering trillions of trillions of individuals, drift from place to place, driven by winds and ocean currents. Light

7

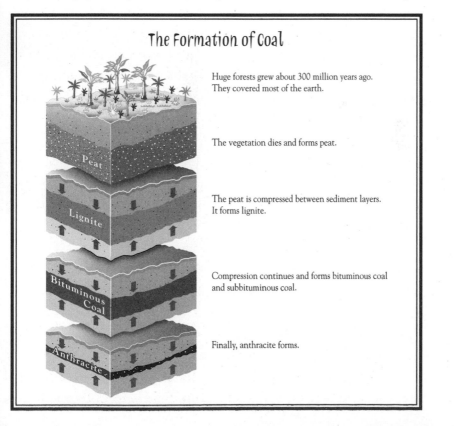

The Formation of Coal

Huge forests grew about 300 million years ago.
They covered most of the earth.

The vegetation dies and forms peat.

The peat is compressed between sediment layers.
It forms lignite.

Compression continues and forms bituminous coal
and subbituminous coal.

Finally, anthracite forms.

Peat

Lignite

Bituminous
Coal

Anthracite

greenish-blue patches, or blooms, of phytoplankton have been photographed from satellites orbiting hundreds of miles above the earth's surface. Called the engine of the sea, phytoplankton form the first link in the food chain. All sea creatures depend on them, and all would die without them. Zooplankton—tiny, immature forms of sea creatures, such as snails, squid, crabs, lobsters, shrimp, and jellyfish—feed on phytoplankton, only to have small fish feed on them. Bigger fish, seabirds, penguins, seals, walruses, polar bears, and whales, in turn, eat small fish. People eat the fish and the larger sea animals. Indirectly, then, people living along seacoasts have always depended upon phytoplankton.

If conditions are right, nature begins to work a chemical miracle on the remains of phytoplankton. When an individual plant dies, it sinks to the ocean floor, where bacteria attack it immediately. Over a few days or weeks, the bacteria make the plant decay into a greasy, carbon-rich material called kerogen. Often, however, the kerogen mixes with mud. Now cut off from oxygen, and thus shielded from bacteria, the kerogen stops decaying. Gradually the kerogen-mud mixture forms a thick carpet, often dozens of feet deep. Layers of sand dropped by rivers cover the carpet. Over time, the ever-thickening sediments bury the mixture deeper and deeper. At a depth of 7,500 to 15,000 feet, it enters what geologists call the oil-gas window.

Two things happen in the oil-gas window. First, as sediments thicken and pressure builds on the lower layers, sand hardens into shale, a rock we can grind up to make bricks and cement. Second, kerogen-rich shale turns into source rock, so called because crude oil and natural gas form inside it.

Deep burial increases pressure, in turn producing heat. Millions of years spent at temperatures of 180 to 280 degrees Fahrenheit "cooks" the kerogen, triggering a complex series of chemical changes that transform it into crude oil and natural gas. Crude oil forms at depths of between 7,500 and 10,500 feet. Natural gas forms at 10,500 to 15,000 feet. Kerogen buried below the oil-gas window gets too hot and is destroyed.

Although formed from the same material, crude oil and natural gas are very different. Crude oil is a liquid under pressure. Carbon accounts for about 80 percent of its weight, and hydrogen about 12 percent; the rest is oxygen, nitrogen, and sulfur. Natural gas is a mixture of gases, but mostly methane. (Methane gas is also produced by cattle. When a cow grazes, bacteria in its stomach aid digestion, breaking down the plant fibers while producing methane as a waste product. Cows give off tremendous amounts of methane—natural gas—through belching and farting.)

Fossil fuels trapped inside source-rock shale do not stay there forever. Since the plates that carry the continents and seabeds constantly shift, they push and pull the source rocks, squeezing out the oil and natural gas. Once freed from their rocky prisons, they can travel long distances underground, often hundreds of miles during millions of years. Because they are lighter than any rocks, they try to move upward through cracks and pores, tiny spaces between the grains of the rocks

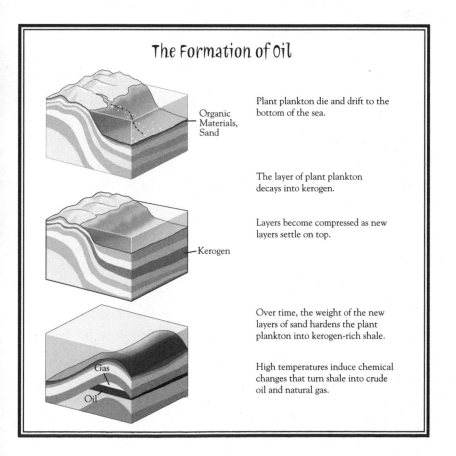

The Formation of Oil

Organic Materials, Sand

Plant plankton die and drift to the bottom of the sea.

The layer of plant plankton decays into kerogen.

Layers become compressed as new layers settle on top.

Kerogen

Over time, the weight of the new layers of sand hardens the plant plankton into kerogen-rich shale.

Gas

Oil

High temperatures induce chemical changes that turn shale into crude oil and natural gas.

above, such as sandstone. These pores often join, forming a network of microscopic channels.

The story of crude oil and natural gas is one of waste, not by humans but by Mother Nature. These fossil fuels eventually rise to the earth's surface. Natural gas then escapes into the air and disappears. Crude oil collects in seeps, or pools, where it leaks onto the ground or into the water. Only 2 percent of "oil spills" in the oceans are from damaged tanker ships; the other 98 percent are from natural seeps. Oil may also trickle down the face of cliffs or ooze through cracks in rocks—thus the name "petroleum," from the Latin for "rock oil" or "oil from the earth." Once exposed to the air, most of it evaporates or is broken down by bacteria.

Just a tiny amount of crude oil and natural gas will ever become useful to us as fuels. For this to happen, these upward-moving fuels must not reach the earth's surface on their own. Instead, they must accumulate in a reservoir formed under a layer of cap rock—that is, a harder type of rock overlaying a softer or weaker rock type. The term "reservoir" is misleading. An oil or gas reservoir is not an underground lake or stream. It is merely a layer of reservoir rock, usually porous sandstone, able to absorb these fuels as a sponge soaks up water. If you drill through the cap rock into a reservoir, the sudden release of pressure, millions of tons per square inch, creates a blowout, or gusher—an uncontrolled release of crude oil or natural gas. A fountain of oil and gas bursts from the ground with a roar, as if you had opened a bottle of soda after giving it a violent shaking.

Explorers have found oil fields on every continent but Antarctica. They have also found them in deep offshore waters, proof that the plates continents ride on have moved over time. Today we live in the age of oil, for without oil and natural gas, our lives would be very different and very poor.

10

II

BLACK GOLD

What a blessing the oil has been to mankind!
—John D. Rockefeller

Oil in Antiquity

The story of people and oil begins in prehistoric times, before the invention of writing. About 40,000 years ago, Stone Age hunters used asphalt to "glue" hand-worked stone points to the shafts of their spears and arrows. Asphalt, also known as bitumen and tar, is crude oil that seeped onto the earth's surface. Upon contact with the air, but before bacteria could decompose it, the oil turned into sticky goo, then hardened. For example, the famous La Brea Tar Pits in Los Angeles, California, are

This painting depicts animals trapped in the La Brea Tar Pits as they might have looked many thousands of years ago.

really asphalt seeps that have turned solid over the centuries. La Brea is a fossil collector's paradise. Preserved in the asphalt are the remains of mammoths, giant elephants that stumbled into the pits and got trapped, along with the saber-toothed tigers that preyed upon them.

Our earliest written records come from the Middle East, known as the cradle of civilization. About 5,000 years ago, people there changed the way they lived. Instead of hunting wild animals and gathering wild plants for food, humans learned to grow crops and keep farm animals. In doing so, they formed the first permanent settlements—towns and cities. The invention of writing allowed farmers to keep track of how much they grew, borrowed, or lent to others, and the taxes they owed their rulers.

Ancient records describe fossil fuels. Writers tell of "eternal fires," natural-gas seeps probably set ablaze by lightning. Such fires do not easily burn themselves out. Some have shot fountains of flaming gas skyward for thousands of years. The Bible tells how Nebuchadnezzar, king of Babylon, plunged three devout Jews into a "fiery furnace" for refusing to worship his golden idol.[1] That furnace still rages near the Iraqi city of Kirkuk, amid one of the world's richest oil fields. During his journey to China in the 1200s, Marco Polo reported "eternal pillars of fire" at Baku on the western shore of the Caspian Sea, later a part of Russia. The roaring flames were so awesome that people believed they must be living gods demanding worship.[2]

Oil served both the living and the dead. Ancient peoples used it as an ointment to treat bruises, sores, and minor cuts. The soldiers of Alexander the Great, while conquering the known world for him, rubbed oil on their scalps to treat rashes caused by their bronze helmets. Arabs, pioneers in chemistry and medicine, praised oil's curative effects. In *The Book of the Powers of Remedies*, written in AD 683, an Arab physician wrote: "Warm naphtha [oil], especially water-white naphtha, when ingested in small doses, is excellent for suppressing cough, for asthma, bladder discomfort, and arthritis."[3] Perhaps some people did feel better, but we cannot be sure whether that was because of the treatment or in spite of it. Surely, no physician today would have a patient drink warm oil for any illness.

The ancients used asphalt as a construction material, as important to them as steel and concrete are to us. Egyptians, Greeks, and Romans waterproofed their ships by smearing layers of melted asphalt on the hulls. Most likely, Noah's ark and the basket Pharaoh's daughter used to hide the baby Moses had asphalt waterproofing, too. King Nebuchadnezzar's masons bound together the bricks in the walls of his capital, Babylon, with asphalt mortar. By the year 800, the Muslim founders of Baghdad, capital of today's Iraq, had made their city the wonder of the world; Arabs called it the Jewel of the World. A city of broad avenues, parks, and universities, Baghdad was also the first city to have paved streets. An Arab traveler named Yakut described how workers began by collecting hardened asphalt in woven reed baskets:

> They have large iron kettles placed over cauldrons which they load with known proportions of bitumen, water and sand. Then they light the cauldrons and heat the mixture until the bitumen melts and mixes with the sand while the workers are continually stirring it. When the stirred mixture reaches the right consistency it is poured over the ground as pavement.[4]

13

Modern roads are paved with tarmac, basically the same materials the old-time Baghdadis used.

Asphalt also helped the dead "live" forever. Ancient Egyptians believed in life after death. But to gain eternal life, a corpse had to be mummified—that is, embalmed and dried to prevent decay. Asphalt was a key ingredient in turning a corpse into a mummy; the word comes from *mumiyyah*, Arabic for "asphalt." Since Egypt had little asphalt, merchants traveled to the Dead Sea, in what is today Israel, to trade with the local Arabs for it. The king of Syria, hoping to profit from the trade, sent an army to occupy the area. Furious that a foreign "thief" should control the fate of their dead, the Egyptians sent an army in 312 BC, thus winning history's first war for oil.[5]

Oil was not only a cause of war, but a tool of war. The ancient Persians wrapped oil-soaked rags around arrows, ignited them, and "fired"

The word "mummy" comes from *mumiyyah,* the Arabic word for "asphalt"—a key ingredient in mummifying a corpse.

them at the enemy. The Romans armed their ships with catapults, machines that hurled spears, stones, and firepots hundreds of feet. Firepots were just that: clay pots filled with oil-soaked straw and set ablaze. Upon striking an enemy vessel, the fragile pot broke, splashing flaming oil across wooden decks, canvas sails, and human flesh.

Christian defenders of Constantinople, now Istanbul, capital of Turkey, went further. They invented a terrifying weapon called Greek fire, a devil's brew of oil, sulfur, and secret ingredients that are still a mystery. The Christians armed their warships with brass pumping devices, really the first flamethrowers. Coming within range of an enemy vessel, sailors squirted streams of "liquid fire" at it. Nothing could quench the flames, which even burned on water. A soldier described the weapon's use against a fort:

> This was the fashion of the Greek fire: it came on as broad in front as a vinegar cask, and the tail of fire that trailed behind it was as big as a great spear; and it made such a noise as it came, that it sounded like the thunder of heaven. It looked like a dragon flying through the air. Such a bright light did it cast, that one could see all over the camp as though it were day, by reason of the great mass of fire, and the brilliance of the light that it shed.[6]

14

ⲦⲰⲢⲢⲕⲰ̄Ⲛ· Ⲏⲣⲁⲓⲥⲇⲉ̀ⲕⲁⲓⲧⲟ̄ⲟⲟⲕⲗⲁⲅⲱ̄ⲏ̄ⲣⲱⲟⲗⲱⲓ̈ⲡⲩⲣⲓ̄·

ⲓⲉⲣⲱⲓⲙⲟⲩ ⲡⲩⲣⲡⲟⲗ Ⲧⲟ̄Ⲛ ⲦⲰⲚⲒⲚⲀⲏⲦⲓ̄ϥⲗⲟⲚ·

Warriors in the late eleventh century used "Greek fire," made from oil, sulfur, and some still-secret ingredients, as a lethal tool of battle. This image comes from an illuminated manuscript dated circa twelfth century.

15

This awesome weapon made even the bravest warriors cringe in fear and run for their lives in panic.

Humanity's Quest for Energy

Although oil had various uses in ancient times, producing energy was not one of them. People have two chief energy needs: for work and for lighting. During most of recorded history, human and animal muscles supplied almost all the energy for work. Muscle power pulled plows, planted and harvested crops, dug irrigation canals, and built homes and monuments like the Egyptian pyramids.

More than 2,000 years ago, people in Persia (modern Iran) invented the windmill. The earliest windmills had large wooden paddles to catch the wind. During the Middle Ages, in Holland, builders improved the design, giving the windmill propeller-like blades covered by canvas sails. Windmills supplied the energy to grind wheat into flour for bread and to saw trees into planks for ships and buildings. Waterwheels placed in fast-flowing streams did the same.

Wood was as much a fuel as a building material. People burned it to heat their homes, cook their food, and melt ore to get the metal in it. Yet each energy source had its limitations. Muscles tired quickly.

Wind did not always blow, nor did rivers flow during droughts. Chopping down too many trees destroyed forests.

Coal, not oil, became a substitute for wood. The Chinese had been using coal to replace wood centuries before Marco Polo visited their country. Everywhere the explorer went, he saw "large black stones that are dug from the mountains as veins, which burn like logs." These black stones, he reported, "keep up the fire better than wood does. . . . If you put them on the fire in the evening and make them catch well, I tell you they keep fire all the night so that one finds some in the morning." He added, "So great is the multitude of people, and stoves, and baths, which are continually heated, that the wood could not be enough" in a land where every person bathed "at least three times a week, and in the winter every day if they can do so."[7]

16

At about the same time, coal became important in Europe for the same reason as in China. A thousand years ago, dense forests covered much of the continent. People feared forests as the home of fierce animals and fiercer outlaws, ghosts, goblins, and demons. Yet, driven by the need for firewood and building materials, people overcame their fears. They chopped away until, around the year 1250, the growing scarcity of wood forced them to turn to coal.

Known as black stone, coal was plentiful in Europe. (People with the last name Blackstone are descendants of coal miners or coal merchants.) Often, thick layers of it lay just beneath the

Windmills, like this one with wooden blades, supplied the energy to grind wheat into flour and saw trees into planks for ships and buildings.

ground. Yet it, too, had a problem. As mines deepened, they filled with water. Bailing them out with buckets was too slow; water rose faster than miners could remove it.

Necessity truly is the mother of invention. As the demand for coal rose in the early 1700s, inventors built steam engines to pump the water out of mine shafts. A simple device, the steam engine burned coal to heat a water-filled tank to a boil, creating steam. It is the nature of steam to expand. If it cannot escape from a closed tank, pressure builds until the tank explodes like a cannon shell. A steam engine, however, releases jets of steam so that they strike paddles attached to a wheel, making it turn rapidly. The turning wheel can power a pump to drain a mine shaft, or it can power the engine of a steamboat or railroad train.

Steam engines made the Industrial Revolution possible. Beginning in England in the 1760s, these devices powered all sorts of machinery. Gathering machines at central points, called factories, allowed for the production of clothing, shoes, furniture, pottery, and other useful things in quantities thought impossible until then. It is no wonder that people spoke of King Coal, because it drove the machines that produced the things that made their lives easier and more comfortable. Cheap cotton underwear, for example, was a blessing, for it allowed people to change every day, preventing bacteria from growing, and keeping down body odors. Until then, most people could afford only one pair of woolen or linen drawers at a time, which they wore until they rotted away.

People met their other energy need, for lighting, in various ways. The term "workday" described a reality. For most of recorded history, people worked and studied in daylight. At dusk, work stopped, because people could not see very well. At night, torches, candles, and fireplaces burning wood or coal gave poor light for doing most tasks. In the 1800s, coal gas, made by heating coal in enclosed ovens and piping it into homes and streetlamps, burned brightly but had an awful smell and a nasty habit of exploding. Each year, coal-gas explosions killed hundreds of people in Europe and America.

Whale oil gave the best light. In the early nineteenth century, some 750 ships from the United States alone scoured the oceans, hunting

17

whales. Other countries had whaling ships, too, but the United States had the largest fleet. Whaling was a dangerous occupation. Herman Melville's famous 1851 novel, *Moby-Dick*, is about a whale hunt that ends in disaster when a great white whale turns on its attackers and rams their ship, drowning nearly the entire crew. Usually, though, crewmen killed the whale and cut its blubber—fat—into long, narrow strips. Boiled in huge kettles, the melted blubber fetched up to $2.50 a gallon, too expensive for ordinary people; American factory workers earned about $3 a week. When burned in a lamp, whale oil had a pleasant smell and burned brightly, which made it popular with wealthy and middle-class people for home use and for lighting offices. Unfortunately, large-scale hunting threatened to wipe out many species of large whales, like the sperm whale, within a few decades.

"Colonel" Drake

People needed a safe, abundant, cheap lighting fuel. A Canadian geologist named Abraham Gesner helped meet the need. In 1854, he found a way to extract a clear liquid from coal by heating it. Gesner called the liquid kerosene, from the Greek words for wax and oil. Kerosene burned slowly, with a bright, steady flame, ideal for indoor lighting. An American chemist, Benjamin Stillman Jr., took the Canadian's discovery a step further. Can kerosene be made from petroleum? he asked. After all, coal and oil were both carbon-rich fossil materials. Stillman's experiments proved that it could. Better yet, it was cheaper to make kerosene from oil than from coal. The only problem was finding enough oil in the United States to make it profitable.

Oil was familiar in western Pennsylvania. Over the ages, seeps formed pools on the ground, and creeks often carried blobs of the black stuff as they flowed. For centuries, Native Americans, mostly of the Seneca tribe, had called oil *antonotons*, or "Oh, how much there is!" They used it to soften animal hides and to make the paint they wore during religious ceremonies glisten. Mostly, though, the Seneca prized oil as a medicine. White settlers followed their lead. Since there were few doctors in the frontier areas, they relied on "Seneca oil" to treat illnesses such as deafness, toothaches, stomach upsets, rheumatism, and rashes. They gathered oil by skimming it off ponds or soaking it up in rags. A quart of "medicinal" oil could go a long way.

In 1859, a group of businessmen hoped to find enough oil in Pennsylvania to supply kerosene to city dwellers. Change was in the air. The nation was growing; that year, Oregon became the thirty-third state to join the Union. It was also growing apart. Back east, John Brown and a few followers seized the federal arsenal at Harpers Ferry, Virginia. Brown, a tall man with blazing eyes and the beard of a Bible prophet, saw slavery as the devil's creation. To abolish it, he wanted to use guns taken from the arsenal to start a slave rebellion in the southern states. Brown failed and went to the gallows, but the debate on the morality of slavery grew fiercer. Next year, the election of Abraham Lincoln, who pledged to prevent the spread of slavery into new territories, set the stage for the Civil War.

19

Meanwhile, the businessmen decided to focus their search on Titusville, a village on Oil Creek, a stream known for its oil seeps. To lead the search effort, they hired "Colonel" Edwin L. Drake. In truth, Drake had never been a soldier; his employers made up the title to impress the local farmers. While the "Colonel" knew nothing about oil, he had followed many trades; his last job had been as a railroad conductor. Yet he was smart, ambitious, and a go-getter.

Drake chose a likely spot along Oil Creek, hired workers, and gave out shovels. Digging by hand got them nowhere. Water filled the hole, and the sides caved in. After many tries, and failures, Drake decided to drill for oil.

Drilling was not new in Pennsylvania; work crews traveled from place to place, offering to drill water wells for farmers for a few cents a foot. They used a heavy steel chisel tied to a strong rope attached to a pulley on a pole. Then heave-ho, my lads! Hoisting the chisel by hand, they repeatedly dropped it in the same spot to make a hole, until they struck water. (In ancient China, drillers used a similar method to get brine from underground. Later, they boiled the brine in shallow iron pans to evaporate the water, then harvested the salt left behind to season and preserve their food. In some of the deeper holes they drilled, they found not only brine but oil and natural gas. We do not know what, if anything, they did with the oil. However, they burned natural gas, along with coal, under the iron pans.)

Drake hired a driller named "Uncle Billy" Smith. Together, they decided to build a derrick, or wooden tower, to house their drill string, as they called the chisel and rope. (The derrick takes its name from Thomas Derrick, a famous seventeenth-century English hangman who, instead of dropping a victim from the gallows, devised a beam with pulleys to lift the victim off the ground by a rope around the neck.) Drake then bought an old steam engine to power the drill string. Again, the hole filled with water, and the surrounding soil collapsed into it. Farmers snickered, calling the operation Drake's Folly. He was a "danged fool" on a fool's errand, they said, and would never find oil by drilling. They were wrong.

What Drake did next would make him famous as the father of the petroleum industry. His solution became the model for all future oil-well drilling. It popped into his mind suddenly, as if by magic. Drake

The original Drake oil well in 1861.

bought sections of iron pipe; he called them drive pipe, because he would drive them into the ground with a battering ram made of an oak log. As the lower sections went deeper, he would attach a new section at the top and then run the drill string through the pipe. That way the pipe kept the water out while the drill attacked the rock below.

On August 28, 1859, the drill broke into reservoir rock near the surface, at a depth of sixty-nine feet. Oil bubbled up, flowing at a rate of twenty-five gallons a day. At first, Drake stored it in wooden wash-tubs bought from farmers' wives. When these ran out, he bought up all the used whiskey barrels he could find, each holding forty-two gallons. That set the standard. A barrel of oil always has the same amount as an old-time whiskey barrel.

Ten years earlier, prospectors had found gold in California, beginning the gold rush. Thousands of forty-niners flocked to California in search of the yellow metal. Drake's discovery of the black liquid triggered a black-gold rush. Overnight, land values along Oil Creek

21

The oil derricks at Titusville, Pennsylvania. (c. 1859)

went sky-high. Titusville's population rose from a few hundred to several thousand. The town buzzed with excitement, and smelled to high heaven, thanks to all that oil. "The whole place," a visitor said, "smells like a corps of soldiers when they have diarrhea." Despite the foul odor, some people—the lucky ones—made their fortune. Dances like the American Petroleum Polka and Oil Gallop Fever became the rage. A hit song, "Oil on the Brain," had this verse:

> There's various kind of oil afloat, Cod-liver,
>   Castor, Sweet;
> Which tend to make a sick man well, and set him
>   on his feet.
> But our's a curious feat performs: We jus a well obtain,
> And set the people crazy with "Oil on the brain."[8]

Yet nobody sang about an unexpected benefit. "Good news for whales," a newspaper announced. Black gold provided enough kerosene to end large-scale whaling. In effect, "Colonel" Drake sank the American whaling fleet and saved the giant creatures from extinction. A poor businessman, he died in poverty.[9]

John D. Rockefeller of Standard Oil

Finding petroleum, however, is just the first step in bringing it to consumers. Unlike coal, which is burned pretty much as it comes from the ground, oil must be refined, or purified, before it can be made into useful products.

Refining is done in a refinery. To use the technical term, a refinery is a factory designed for fractional distillation. Crude oil is a mixture of chemicals in various proportions, called fractions, each of which boils at a different temperature. Boiling allows the chemicals to be separated by distillation. Distillation involves heating a liquid until it turns into a vapor and then cooling the vapor until it condenses—that is, turns back into liquid. For example, boiling water turns to vapor—steam— in a teakettle, then condenses back to water when it meets cool air.

A refinery works like a gigantic, more complicated teakettle. The teakettle part, called a fractionating tower, is a tall stainless-steel cylinder with sets of pipes placed horizontally at different levels. As oil boils, vapors rise in the tower. Vapors of the lightest fractions, those with the lowest boiling points, rise higher and cool faster than heavier fractions with higher boiling points. Making their way upward, the condensed liquids flow into the pipes placed at their level, then flow into storage tanks on the ground. Naphtha forms at the tower's topmost level. Used in laundry soaps, home-cleaning fluids, shoe polish, varnish, and camping stoves, refiners also mix naphtha with gasoline, which forms on the level just below it. Kerosene, jet-plane fuel, and diesel oil—which is used to power locomotives, large trucks, and ships—form at midlevel. The chief lower-level liquids are home heating oil and lubricating oil, used to prevent the moving parts of machines from wearing out as they rub against each other. Tar and thick waste oil called sludge form at the very bottom of the tower.

Nowadays, a typical refinery has scores of fractionating towers, hundreds of miles of pipes, and huge clusters of storage tanks. It never completely shuts down, although sections are always being taken offline for routine cleaning, maintenance, and repairs. However, the

23

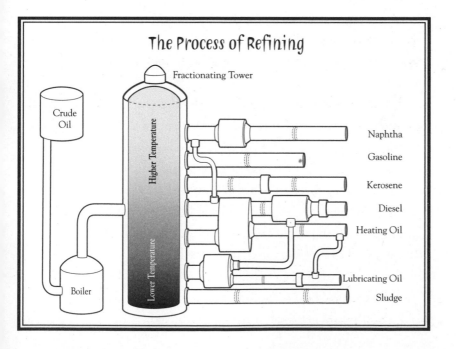

The Process of Refining

Fractionating Tower

Crude Oil

Higher Temperature

Lower Temperature

Boiler

Naphtha

Gasoline

Kerosene

Diesel

Heating Oil

Lubricating Oil

Sludge

refinery as a whole operates rain or shine, day and night, every day of the year. It covers an area the size of dozens of football fields and employs as many as 2,000 workers in three eight-hour shifts. Not every worker refines oil, though. A refinery, they say, is a fire waiting to happen. Thus, each has a complete fire department, teams of experts who do nothing but stand by, ready to put out fires at a moment's notice.

While oil played no role in the outcome of the Civil War, by the time the conflict ended in 1865, refining oil into kerosene had become a big business. Oil made what would grow into America's largest firm, the Standard Oil Company, not only an economic force but a power in government, politics, and foreign affairs. The American oil industry as we know it today is largely the creation of John D. Rockefeller, Standard Oil's founder.

Rockefeller was born in upstate New York in 1839 and died in 1937. His father, William "Big Bill" Rockefeller, was a traveling salesman and small-time swindler. His mother, Eliza, was a devout, long-suffering housewife. Young John did not admire his father and resolved to be as unlike him as possible. Deeply religious like his mother, he believed everything good that came to him was a gift from God. Rockefeller explained:

> Early I learned to work and to play. I dropped the
> worry on the way. God was good to me every day.[10]

Out of gratitude to God, all his life Rockefeller gave as much as he could afford, eventually hundreds of millions of dollars, to churches, charities, universities, and medical research. A loyal friend and a devoted husband, he enjoyed singing, telling ghost stories, and playing with his children. Everyone laughed at his favorite trick of balancing a cracker on the tip of his nose and catching it in his mouth as it fell.

The American people came to see Rockefeller as two people—one with an angel's halo, the other with devil's horns. The man with the halo believed that God gave him his money so that he could do good. The man with the horns was ruthless; mothers told their children that Rockefeller would get them if they misbehaved.

Rockefeller loved money. Even as a child, he recalled, "I determined to make money work for me."[11] A fast learner, he had a knack for business. For example, as a youngster he bought candy by the pound in a local grocery. This he divided into small portions, which he sold to neighbors at a profit. He also had a way with numbers, doing complicated problems instantly in his head. At age fifteen, he quit school to seek his fortune first as a bookkeeper, at fifty cents a day, then as a grain merchant. Yet he always managed to put aside money for charity and to invest. Finally, in his midtwenties, he decided that the road to riches led to the oil industry.

Oil offered opportunity for a hard-driving man like Rockefeller. As the demand for kerosene rose, the smell of crude oil began to smell like cold cash. It seemed to drive people out of their minds. Eager to get rich quickly, hundreds headed every year for Pennsylvania and the oil fields discovered in neighboring states after the Civil War.

25

Oil was a wasteful, dog-eat-dog business, driven by greed. The industry cared no more about the damage it did to the environment than did the hunters who, at the time, were slaughtering buffalo for their hides. Eager for a quick profit at any cost, those whose wells "came in" often wasted more oil than they sold. With oil so plentiful, they allowed thousands of barrels to flow into creeks; the Allegheny River stank of oil and rotting fish, killed because the oil prevented them from getting oxygen from the water. Some fools grew impatient with drilling. They decided to rush

John D. Rockefeller was known as both a generous philanthropist and a ruthless businessman. Mothers warned their children that if they misbehaved, Rockefeller would get them. (c. 1909)

things by tossing nitroglycerine, a high explosive, down drill holes, killing everyone nearby. (Once, the lone survivor of such an explosion stood dazed and naked, having lost every stitch of clothing and strand of hair on his body.) Competition became so fierce that prices rose and fell wildly. In 1862, for example, a barrel of oil fell from $4 to 35 cents and then jumped to $13.75. Worse, refiners cut corners in making kerosene. Lamps filled with impure kerosene exploded, killing scores of people each year. In 1880, kerosene lamps caused 39 percent of New York City fires.[12]

The oil industry, then, was a savage brawl. Success in it, Rockefeller saw, lay not in finding black gold but in refining a superior product and selling it cheaply, at a fixed price. In 1863, as the Civil War raged, he and four partners built a refinery in Cleveland, Ohio. Calling their firm the Standard Oil Company was no accident. The name suggested a standard quality of kerosene that consumers could trust not to turn family and home to ashes.

Pure kerosene, Rockefeller insisted, was a blessing. It meant people could read more, learn more, and thus make progress as never before. In short, by providing the best kerosene cheaply, Rockefeller believed he was serving God while making his fortune. He saw God's hand in Standard Oil's growing profits. An employee once passed Rockefeller's office and saw, through the open door, the boss jumping up and down while clicking his heels. "I'm bound to be rich!" he shouted, overcome with joy. "Bound to be rich! *Bound to be rich!*"[13]

To get rich, Rockefeller vowed to "bring order" to the oil industry. That meant eliminating all competition. He began by making Standard Oil a model of efficiency. Pennies counted, for, like Benjamin Franklin, he believed that a penny saved is a penny earned. The boss cut costs wherever possible. Take wooden barrels, which sold for $2.50 apiece. Rockefeller had Standard Oil's barrels made for 96 cents apiece. He did this by buying his own tracts of oak timber, sawmills, and assembly shops. Then he plowed the savings back into Standard Oil to buy better equipment to produce better kerosene at even lower cost.

When it came to beating the competition, Rockefeller was not squeamish. He could be tough, even dishonest, in gaining an advantage.

26

When he decided to take over a rival company, he offered to buy out the owners at a "fair price"—that is, his price. If they refused, he sent spies to discover the company's strengths and weaknesses. He then used the information to make the owners "feel sick."

"Sickness" took many forms. Rockefeller cut the price of kerosene to the point competitors could not match and stay in business. He also secretly got railroads to give rebates, or money back, on freight charges in return for a guaranteed amount of business. Since rivals paid regular rates, they could not match Standard Oil's prices.

Rockefeller went further, creating the trust, a group of companies united by him to monopolize the oil-refining industry. The Standard Oil Trust bought rivals out, adding their production to its own. By the early 1880s, Rockefeller controlled 90 percent of the oil refined in the United States; kerosene accounted for more of the nation's overseas trade than any other product. Moreover, Rockefeller controlled most of the nation's pipelines and railroad tank cars. Giant sugar, meatpacking, steel, tobacco, and life-insurance companies soon formed trusts in their industries. Eventually, Rockefeller became the first American to have a personal fortune of a billion dollars. Rich as he was, the oil tycoon faced two grave challenges: one from a genius, the other from a politician.

The first challenge came from Thomas A. Edison. The brilliant inventor believed that science must come out of the laboratory and into the marketplace. "We have got to keep working up things of commercial value—that is what this laboratory is for," he wrote.[14] In his laboratories, Edison set teams of scientists and engineers to work on practical, everyday problems. Under his guidance, they invented the phonograph and improved the telegraph, telephone, and motion pictures. Their most important invention, however, was the electric lightbulb, first demonstrated to the public in 1879. The oil industry soon felt the effects of the "new light." Yet Rockefeller's luck held. For as kerosene sales fell, another invention, the automobile, saved the day.

Building an average-size car used the energy of twenty barrels (840 gallons) of oil. The vehicle itself got the power to move from the internal combustion engine, which burns a mixture of fuel and air. That fuel, gasoline, created a new market for petroleum.

Thomas Edison, seen here experimenting in his laboratory, first demonstrated the lightbulb to the public in 1879.

28

Gasoline is the largest fraction of a refined barrel of oil. One forty-two-gallon barrel yields 19.4 gallons of gasoline. Before the automobile, gasoline had little practical use. Although grocers sold it in small bottles as cleaning fluid to remove stains from clothing and lice from hair, refiners thought it a nuisance. This "waste product" of making kerosene usually wound up in the nearest stream. Rockefeller recalled how "thousands and hundreds of thousands of barrels of it floated down the creeks and rivers, and the ground was saturated with it, in the constant effort to get rid of it."[15] So much gasoline was dumped that a stray match or cigarette could turn miles of river into an inferno. Even so, gasoline made Standard Oil larger, richer, and more powerful than most state governments. By the 1890s, Standard Oil controlled scores of railroads, bridges, steamships, copper mines, and foreign oil companies, particularly in South America. It had its own "army" of security guards, larger than most state police forces or national guards.

Just as Rockefeller believed God gave him his money to do good works, he believed that money talks. This made Standard Oil a threat to democracy. There is a difference between ethical lobbying—trying to persuade lawmakers by appealing to logic and their sense of right and wrong to vote or act in a certain way—and buying their loyalty. Rockefeller had no objection to bribing politicians if that was needed to get what he wanted. Politicians, a Standard Oil official explained,

> come in here and ask us to contribute to their campaign funds. And we do it. . . . We put our hands in our pockets and give them some good sums for campaign purposes and then when a bill comes up that is against our interest we . . . say: "There's such and such a bill up. We don't like it and we want you to take care of our interests."[16]

Other giant companies acted in the same way. The only losers were the American people.

A famous cartoon illustrated Rockefeller's political power. In it, the master of Standard Oil has turned the U.S. Capitol into an oil refinery, with chimneys spewing waste gases into the air. Rockefeller

29

The famous cartoon portraying Rockefeller controlling the government, originally published in *The Verdict* on January 22, 1900.

President Theodore Roosevelt was often described as a "steamroller in trousers." (c. 1911)

holds the White House in one hand. As he turns it over, the president and his cabinet come tumbling out. "What a funny little government," says Rockefeller. "Funny" because he and his partners, lawyers, and managers had more to say in running it than voters did.

Rockefeller's second challenge came from the twenty-sixth president of the United States. Described as "a steamroller in trousers," Theodore Roosevelt was a forceful man who believed that our democracy could not survive if the rich bought politicians to get their way. TR, as everyone called him, felt it his duty to do anything for the public good, unless forbidden by law. The Sherman Antitrust Act, passed by Congress in 1890 to end unfair competition, became his chief weapon. Nicknamed "the Trustbuster," TR ordered the Department of Justice to break up trusts in several industries, including railroads.

Rockefeller headed the president's list of "malefactors of great wealth," criminals who used money to corrupt government, a problem that still exists. Another famous cartoon, titled "The Infant Hercules and the Standard Oil Serpents," expressed Roosevelt's attitude. It showed a naked baby Hercules—TR—wearing a mustache and eyeglasses, wrestling snakes with the faces of Rockefeller and an unidentified aide. Three years after the president left office in 1908, the Supreme Court ruled against Standard Oil, allowing the breakup plan to go forward. The giant oil company became thirty-four new companies, some of which are still household names. These companies included Standard Oil of New Jersey, later called Exxon; Standard Oil

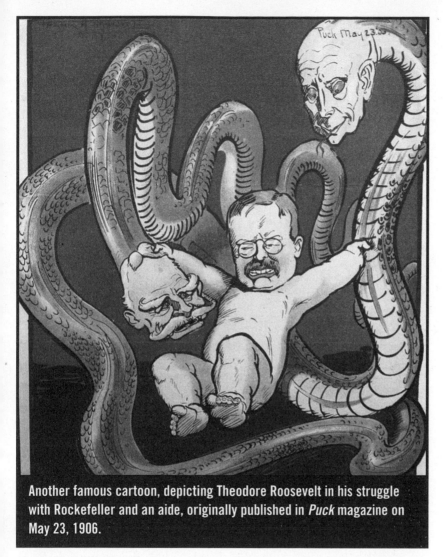

Another famous cartoon, depicting Theodore Roosevelt in his struggle with Rockefeller and an aide, originally published in *Puck* magazine on May 23, 1906.

of New York, later renamed Mobil, then ExxonMobil; Standard Oil of Indiana, the future Amoco; and Continental Oil, later Conoco. Since Rockefeller owned stock in the new companies, he became richer than ever.

The economic growth spurred by the oil industry continued. Even as the Supreme Court ruled against Standard Oil, black gold had become a force on the world stage—literally a driving force of history.

III

THE DESTINY OF NATIONS

Oil has played a unique role in the economy and history of modern times. No other raw material has been so critical in shaping the destiny of nations.

—*Leonardo Maugeri*
Director of Strategies and Development for EniSpA,
a leading international oil and gas company

Making an Oil Well

As the twentieth century began, the growing market for black gold spurred the search for new ways to find and produce it. The making of an oil well followed a set pattern, developed quickly through trial and error and lots of luck. Oil has never been a business for the timid, but for risk takers willing to put their money, and sometimes their lives, on the line.

Before anything, searchers had to find a likely place to drill. Like Colonel Drake, many did the obvious: they set up shop at known oil seeps. Yet that did not guarantee success, for a seep might point only to a thin layer of reservoir rock below. Other explorers tried various sorts of mumbo jumbo. Some, called "doodle-buggers," searched with a doodlebug, a small black box holding a tube of oil attached to a string. Supposedly, the box would start swinging if its owner walked, ever so slowly, over an oil reservoir. "Hot-footers" got hot feet when they walked over an oil deposit. "Old-hatters" tossed an old hat into the air and drilled wherever it landed. Even so, some found oil, not because of their method, but because of blind luck.

Soon university-educated geologists began to take charge of exploration. Although still unable to "see" underground, they relied on clues found on the surface. Studying the lay of the land, they drew detailed maps showing domes, or bulges, in otherwise flat ground. Domes pointed to possible formations of cap rock covering oil reservoirs hundreds, even thousands, of feet below the surface. When the geologists finished their studies, the real work began.

Work crews built an access road, cleared the land, and set up a derrick, or rig, for the drill. Colonel Drake's drill string was simply a heavy steel chisel raised by a pulley and repeatedly dropped in the same spot. But by the early 1900s, the drill string had a fast-spinning drill powered by an electric motor that rotated it like a giant dentist's drill; we call this the rotary system of drilling. Then, as now, the drill's cutting end was a bit tipped with up to 1,600 industrial diamonds— that is, diamonds not suited for use in jewelry. The diamond, the purest form of carbon, is the hardest substance on Earth; it can cut anything found in nature. A drill bit's diamond teeth are set into three cone-shaped steel blades, called cutters, that spin separately, but at the same speed and in the same direction. The best-quality bits may cost over $300,000 and last 100 hours before requiring replacement.

33

A drill bit used in the rotary system of drilling.

Clearly, drilling an oil well is a very expensive proposition.

Workers begin drilling into the ground. When the bit hits solid rock, they remove it and insert thirty-foot sections of steel pipe, slightly smaller in diameter than the drill hole, called casing. Each section of casing has threads like those of a screw at either end, and it is installed by flinging a chain around it. After workers fit the threads of each new section of pipe to those on the one beneath, they tighten them with a super-large wrench called tongs. Having secured the lengths of casing, they fill the gap between them and the drill hole with cement to prevent the hole from caving in. Finally, they lower the bit into the pipe and continue drilling.

As the bit spins, the crew pumps a mixture of liquefied clay and chemicals, called drilling mud, into the casing pipe. The bit's spinning motion circulates the mud, cooling the bit and bringing chunks of rock to the surface. From time to time, the crew pulls the bit out of the deepening hole, adds more casing pipe and cement, and then reinserts the bit. The crew repeats this tedious job every 200 feet or so.

A gusher in Port Arthur, Texas, in 1901.

Should the bit break off its mounting and drop to the bottom of the hole, workers must fish it out with a powerful magnet.

With luck, the bit will strike oil after only a few days, at a depth of several hundred feet. Yet it often takes weeks, with the bit reaching depths of 17,500 feet (over three miles). If no oil is found by then, the boss declares a "duster" or "dry hole"—no oil. In other words, all money and effort spent were for nothing.

Striking oil, however, was at once an exciting and a terrifying experience. In the early days of deep-well drilling, the sudden release of pressure in the reservoir rock triggered a blowout, or gusher. Gushers announced themselves with a rumbling noise; some imagined it as the growling of a great beast chained beneath the earth for ages. The ground shook. Moments later, a torrent of oil, gas, mud, and sand erupted from the ground. Shooting up the center of the derrick, it leaped hundreds of feet into the air. An old-timer remembered:

> We immediately got cotton and stuffed our ears. It was very
> deafening, you couldn't hear anybody talk, you had to
> make hand signals. There was sand coming down all over
> us, blasting at us, and the rig became shiny in about two
> hours. All the paint was stripped off of it, and all the rust
> and everything.[1]

While gushers were awesome sights, they wasted oil and killed people. A worker recalled how

> three thousand feet of pipe just went right up and out, just
> like a big string of macaroni, and it curved over and hit the
> ground and flopped over into big coils. This was solid pipe,
> you know, about five inches thick. And this guy got hit by
> one of these flopping coils, and was killed. [Another guy]
> outran it by a few feet. He damn near got it![2]

By the late 1930s, engineers had learned how to control gushers with a special shutoff device called a Christmas tree, or blowout

35

preventer, a series of valves that relieved pressure slowly, then cut off the flow altogether. Preventing gushers not only saves oil and lives but protects the environment. Oil from a runaway gusher can flood the land for miles around, polluting streams and poisoning the soil so that nothing can grow.

Texas Giants

New drilling methods opened new areas of the United States to exploration. Prospectors struck it rich in California and Louisiana. The most important find, however, was the Spindletop oil field.

Located in southeastern Texas, about thirty miles inland from the Gulf of Mexico, Spindletop took its name from a small hill that stood out on the flat coastal plain near the town of Beaumont. At its crown, the hill had a tree shaped like a child's spinning top. According to a Native American legend, ghosts haunted Spindletop; they danced by the light of the moon and angrily chased away trespassers.

Nothing could chase Pattillo Higgins away. A self-taught geologist, Higgins was a lumber dealer who had lost an arm in a saloon shoot-out. During visits to Spindletop, Higgins realized that the hill was really a dome and that oil must lie in reservoir rock beneath the surface. When he said so, townspeople joked that if old Higgins thought there was oil, then let him get it out. Since he could not afford to drill on his own, he advertised in a magazine for someone to put up the cash. Only one reply came, from Captain Anthony F. Lucas, a trained mining engineer.

36

Pattillo Higgins correctly believed that oil lay under a domed hill in Spindletop, Texas. (c. 1900–1910)

The oil derricks at Spindletop. (c. 1915)

37

Lucas had the needed money and began drilling with the new rotary system.

January 10, 1901, is a key day in oil history. Moments after sunrise, the ground beneath the derrick began to tremble, and mud bubbled up through the casing pipe. The trembling came from a depth of 1,020 feet, growing more violent by the minute. Suddenly tons of casing pipe shot over the top of the derrick, followed by a gusher that flew 200 feet into the air.

"Oil, oil on the hill," shouted the citizens of Beaumont, amazed at the sight. Men leaped onto their horses and sped toward the gusher. "People are saying you're the wisest man on Earth. Hell, ain't you surprised?" a rider called to Higgins. "Not exactly," he replied. He'd known there was oil under Spindletop all along.[3]

Spindletop gushed more than 100,000 barrels of oil that day, more than any seen at one time in human history. The Texas oil boom had begun. By year's end, 225 wells, placed a few feet apart, were producing record amounts of oil. Between the years 1901 and 2000, the Spindletop field yielded more than 155 million barrels of oil. Texans vowed to protect their bonanza from "that damn Yankee" John D. Rockefeller. And they succeeded, thanks to contacts in the state government, bribes to legislators, and generous gifts to political campaigns. Spindletop made the United States the world's greatest oil producer. It also gave birth to companies as large as, or larger than, any of Rockefeller's after the breakup of Standard Oil. These included Texas Oil (later Texaco), Gulf Oil, Cities Service, Humble Oil, and Amoco.[4]

Spindletop became the "school" of the oil industry. American oil workers spread worldwide the tricks of the trade they learned there. These men saw themselves as a breed apart, bold adventurers like cowboys, lumberjacks, and sailors. "The drilling business," one told an interviewer, "is a very macho environment. It's a rough, tough life."[5]

Ranging in age from their late teens to their early thirties, oil workers were strong and energetic, willing to challenge death each time they came to the job. "A drilling rig is a little bit of hell on Earth," a retired oilman recalled, "a small, crowded space that is terrifying to the outsider." A fellow worker added, "There are chains flying around, and pipe swinging here and there, and terrible noises. . . . People get hurt. Things break. Guys fall out of derricks, nearly a hundred feet to the floor. Quite a few people die."[6]

After working hard, oil workers played hard. "There was a lot of horseplay," said a veteran. "Like, a guy would be sound asleep. And these guys would go get a high-pressure water hose and stick it in his pants." Or they would set fire to the seat of a sleeping man's pants—"that was a favorite trick."[7]

On days off, workers "went to town," if there was one nearby, to gamble, drink, fight, and flirt with women. They had their own language, too. A "wildcatter" searched for oil in places no one else expected to find any. A "driller" was top man on the job; he took charge of boring the well. A skilled helper was a "roughneck." The name, one explained, came from the fact that men who worked on rigs often bent their heads backward to see what was going on above. "Because

38

of looking up a lot, you'd develop wrinkles in the back of your neck, and consequently the name 'roughneck' was developed." A common laborer was a "roustabout," the same as a circus worker who sets up and takes down tents and does other odd jobs.[8]

Mr. Churchill Builds a Modern Navy

As the derricks rose in Texas, war planners had already shown interest in black gold. The opening years of the twentieth century were a trying time, one of gathering war clouds. European nations wanted markets for their manufactured goods in Asia and Africa, as well as colonies to produce the raw materials their factories needed to make those goods. Fierce competition presented military men with the question of how to defend national interests across wide oceans, thousands of miles from the homeland.

In the twenty-first century, nations project power with long-range bombers, troop transports, ballistic missiles, nuclear submarines, and aircraft carriers. A century ago, nations defended, and furthered, their interests with battleships. Known as capital ships, these were a navy's most important vessels, the key to sea power. A nation without battle-ships counted for little in world affairs.

Battleships have a long history. The first ones, built in the 1500s, were wooden vessels powered by wind and sails, armed with cannons that fired iron balls half a mile. By the 1860s, during the American Civil War, small iron ships driven by steam engines, like the USS *Monitor*, fired explosive shells about a mile. Forty years later, the aver-age battleship measured 350 feet in length by 70 feet wide. It fired a 1,100-pound explosive shell a distance of ten miles.

Such battleships needed a 500-man crew, officers and sailors, to manage them on the high seas. Yet anywhere from one-quarter to one-third of the crew had nothing to do with sailing or shooting. They handled the coal (anthracite) and worked the boilers that made steam for the engines. Shipmates called them the black gang, because coal dust covered every exposed inch of flesh. Dust got into their pores, turning skin a deep blue-black; sailors tattooed one another by prick-ing their skin with pins and rubbing fine dust particles into the holes.

Each black gang had "passers," who hauled heavy coal sacks aboard and emptied them down chutes into storage bins below. "Stokers" shoveled coal into the boilers. Wearing only drawers and shoes, bodies glistening with sweat, stokers worked in temperatures of 170 degrees Fahrenheit and above. Working steadily, they paused only to thrust their heads into tubs of water placed beside each boiler. Sometimes the heat from the boilers made them pass out.

Great Britain lived because of the sea. The island nation had to sell what it made overseas so it could buy what it needed. To survive, it even had to import large quantities of food, particularly meat and wheat from the United States and South America. For three centuries, the Royal Navy supported British armies in the colonies—especially India, the most valuable—and in Egypt, through which the Suez Canal passes. The canal enabled the Royal Navy, the world's largest, to rush reinforcements anywhere and keep trade flowing along the sea-lanes. This made other nations jealous.

Many Germans felt their country deserved to be regarded as a key world power. This, in turn, meant that German industry needed vast quantities of raw materials—cotton, rubber, copper, tin, aluminum—from overseas. Since Britain had the most profitable colonies, German leaders realized it would not willingly surrender its advantage. Germany aimed, then, at threatening Britain by building a High Seas Fleet to rival the Royal Navy. So, in the years after 1897, German shipyards launched the biggest and fastest battleships ever seen. If things continued this way, Germany would soon master the world's seas. Clearly, the British Empire was living on borrowed time.

Winston Churchill understood the danger. The son of an English nobleman and his American wife, Churchill was a jack-of-all-trades: adventurer, soldier, newspaper reporter, historian, and politician. Today he is famous for leading Britain to victory during World War II. In 1911, however, Churchill had only recently launched his political career. In that year, he became First Lord of the Admiralty, the Royal Navy's civilian chief. If Germany continued to build its fleet, Churchill feared, his country would become helpless, a poor, starving little island without hope. How to catch up?

Britain still had the world's largest fleet, but size is not the same as quality. Most of its warships were old, slow, outdated—sitting ducks for the High Seas Fleet. Churchill decided to make a technological leap forward. He would scrap the older ships, hundreds of them, using the money saved on their upkeep to build super-battleships.

Called the *Queen Elizabeth* class, these vessels would burn oil. While Britain had the best ship-grade coal in the world, coal had problems. Coal-burning ships were nearly impossible to

Winston Churchill embraced new technologies early on in his political career. (c. 1915)

41

refuel at sea and gave off clouds of smoke, visible at long distances to enemy lookouts. Oil was a far superior fuel. While it occupied less space than coal, it packed twice the energy. This meant that the space used for coal storage could be given over to thicker armor plate and longer-range guns. A *Queen Elizabeth*–class battleship was 646 feet long by 91 feet wide. Each of its nine main guns could hurl a 2,000-pound shell twenty-one miles. Out of a crew of 1,300, only a few dozen tended the boilers; the rest handled the vessel and fought. Churchill explained:

> An oil-burning fleet can . . . keep its station at sea,
> nourishing itself from tankers without having to send
> a quarter of its strength continually into harbour to coal,
> wasting fuel on the homeward and outward journey. The
> ordeal of coaling ship exhausted the whole ship's company.
> In wartime it robbed them of their brief period of rest; it
> subjected everyone to extreme discomfort. With oil, a few
> pipes were connected . . . with a tanker and the ship sucked
> in its fuel with hardly a man having to lift a finger.[9]

Oil-burning *Queen Elizabeth*–class battleships had an edge over Germany's coal-burning ships. (c. 1918)

Churchill's decision to convert to oil gave the Royal Navy an important edge in fighting Germany's coal-burning battleships.

His decision, however, seemed like a reckless gamble. For a 3,000-mile voyage, a *Queen Elizabeth*–class battleship would need enough fuel to heat a medium-size family home for five centuries! Yet Churchill ordered building to begin before solving the oil-supply problem, a highly risky *and* courageous move. Britain bought its oil from the United States, the Dutch East Indies (today's Indonesia), and the Baku fields in Russia; the nearby city, also called Baku,

Winston Churchill's foresight that oil would be a key factor in World Wars I and II helped lead the Allied forces to victory. (date unknown)

was known as the Black City because showers of oil droplets from gushers often rained down on it. Britain could not afford to depend on foreigners, even friendly ones, for this vital resource. It needed its own oil supply, one it could control and buy at a low price. Churchill turned his eyes toward the Middle East.

Written records had mentioned crude-oil seeps, asphalt, and natural-gas fires in the Middle East since ancient times. Yet nobody knew where to find oil in large quantities, let alone had drilled a well anywhere in the region. Besides, Islam was the official religion of the Middle Eastern countries. Like all people, followers of Islam, or Muslims, have historically been suspicious of foreigners. Devout Muslims felt that Europeans—mostly Christians and Jews—were infidels, scheming unbelievers.

One place, though, seemed likely to have plenty of oil and a Muslim ruler willing to cooperate for the right price. A dynasty, or series of rulers who belong to the same family, of shahs—emperors—ruled Persia (today's Iran), and this particular dynasty was corrupt. Shahs imagined themselves as superhuman beings; almost godlike, they gave themselves grand titles such as "Ruler of Rulers" and "Conqueror of Lands." Anyone who refused to honor the shah might be whipped to death, shot from a cannon, buried alive, or burned in a town square. To support their lavish lifestyles, shahs sold concessions—licenses— to foreigners, whatever their religion. A concession gave the buyer, and that buyer alone, the right to sell a product or service in Persia. Foreigners ran the country's telephone and telegraph systems, railroads, banks, and industries, even printed its money and postage stamps.

A visitor described Persia's Shah Muzzaffar al-Din as "merely an elderly child" who talked baby talk and lived for pleasure alone. Word of the shah's money troubles reached William Knox D'Arcy, a millionaire who had struck it rich in the Australian goldfields. Yet D'Arcy was not satisfied; he wanted to make a fortune in black gold, too, becoming the John D. Rockefeller of the Middle East. In 1901, just as oil poured from the Spindletop field, D'Arcy persuaded Shah Muzzaffar to sell him the right to search for, produce, refine, and sell Persian oil.[10]

D'Arcy learned that finding oil was more expensive, and frustrating, than he had imagined. His work crews had to haul drilling equipment long distances, across rugged, roadless country. Arriving at a likely site, they drilled holes, plenty of them, but found nothing. When D'Arcy began to run out of money, he located partners in Scotland to share the costs. Still, no oil! It seemed as if they were pouring money down rat holes. D'Arcy and the other investors decided to give up before they lost everything.

On May 24, 1908, a message arrived from Scotland for George Reynolds, D'Arcy's driller. "Cease work," it said, "dismiss the staff, dismantle anything worth the cost of transporting to the coast for re-shipment, and come home."[11] Reynolds disobeyed. He felt that he needed just a few more days to find oil. And he was right. Two days after the message arrived, he struck oil at Masjid-i-Suleiman in western Persia.

Masjid-i-Suleiman became a second Spindletop. One well after another gushed black gold. British engineers and Persian laborers built a 130-mile pipeline, the first in the Middle East, at Abadan, a desert island at the northern end of the Persian Gulf, a narrow body of water between Iran and the Arabian Peninsula. From Abadan, tankers could carry the oil to markets everywhere. Workers for the newly formed Anglo-Persian Oil Company hated Abadan, described as a place of "mud, flies and stifling heat."[12] Abadan would become the largest oil refinery on Earth, but not until the 1920s.

Meanwhile, Winston Churchill made his gamble pay off. Iranian oil, he said, was "a prize from fairyland beyond our wildest dreams."[13] In June 1914, at his request, the British government bought a controlling share in D'Arcy's company. A secret agreement allowed the Royal Navy to buy oil at bargain prices. But it was a close call, because two months after the purchase, war broke out in Europe.

Oil Goes to War

People called it the Great War, the World War, and the First World War. Not that they believed, then, that there would be a second world war. They used the term "First World War" because it was the first war fought on a worldwide scale. On one side stood the Central Powers:

Germany, Austria-Hungary, Bulgaria, and Turkey. Ranged against them were the Allies. These included France, Russia, Belgium, Italy, Japan, and the British Empire—Great Britain, India, Canada, Australia, New Zealand, South Africa. Humanity had never brought such a disaster upon itself.

Britain acted quickly to secure its oil supply. In the fall of 1914, it sent an army from India to seize Basra, a city on the mainland, near Abadan. Back then, Basra was in Mesopotamia, the ancient Land of the Two Rivers, the Tigris and Euphrates, and belonged to Germany's ally, Turkey.

Meanwhile, in Europe, German armies advanced across Belgium into France. In fierce fighting, French forces halted the onslaught, but they had to leave the northern part of their country in enemy hands. To prevent the invader from pushing farther, or to keep the land they had already taken, each side dug deep trenches. Lines of trenches, one behind the other, stretched from France's border with Switzerland across Belgium to the North Sea, a distance of some five hundred miles.

The war bogged down, with neither side able to strike a knockout blow. For millions of soldiers, life became a hellish nightmare. Massed

45

A quiet moment in the German trenches during World War I. (c. 1916)

artillery rained high-explosive shells on the opposing trench lines. Artillery, rifles, and machine guns slaughtered attacking forces. Clouds of poison gas blinded soldiers, burned their skin, and seared their lungs, slowly choking them to death as their skin turned purple for lack of oxygen. "Humanity is mad!" a French officer wrote in his diary shortly before his death. "It must be mad to do what it is doing. What a massacre! What scenes of horror and bloodshed! Hell cannot be so terrible. Men are mad!"[14]

As the madness continued, each side searched for ways to break the deadlock. Their search always involved petroleum. This was because, for the first time in history, war depended on oil and gasoline-powered machines.

At sea, Britain's oil-burning battleships forced Germany's coal-burning High Seas Fleet to retreat to its bases and stay there for fear of being destroyed. On land, fleets of trucks ferried supplies and troops to the front. Flamethrowers shot streams of burning gasoline—modern Greek fire—at enemy soldiers. Occasionally an accident or a stray bullet turned a flamethrower carrier into a living torch. Heavy vehicles, powered by gasoline and armed with light cannons, tried to overrun the enemy positions, only to get bogged down in mud and blown apart by artillery. A British invention, these vehicles are still called by the code name Winston Churchill gave them while they were being secretly developed: tanks.

Gasoline also powered another weapon, the airplane. Built by the Wright brothers, Orville and Wilbur, of Dayton, Ohio, the first airplane took off from the beach at Kitty Hawk, North Carolina, on December 17, 1903. Peace-loving men, the brothers expected their invention to serve humanity in a unique way. By bringing people closer together, the airplane would help them understand each other better, thus eliminating wars. They were wrong, for the airplane became a fearsome weapon. At first used to locate enemy ground positions, it quickly developed into a fighter and bomber.

The warplane of World War I was simple, slow (top speed seventy-five miles an hour), flimsy, and deadly—not just to the enemy, but to the pilot, too. To save weight, its body was a wooden frame held

A Royal Flying Corps Sopwith Camel, used by British forces during World War I. (c. 1917)

47

together by steel wires. A canvas skin covered the body, coated with "dope," a varnish waterproofer that easily caught fire. Ground crews made repairs with wire clippers, scissors, and glue. The pilot sat in an open cockpit. His seat, made of flammable wicker, rested above the gasoline tank and fuel lines leading to the engine. In effect, he rode an incendiary bomb.

A pilot's worst fear was death by gasoline, not bullets. Getting hit by a string of machine-gun bullets brought instant death, probably painlessly. To burn alive was the most horrible fate a pilot could imagine. The pilots' nicknames for gasoline captured their fears: "Orange Death," "Hell-brew," "Witches' Water," "Infernal Liquid." A pilot was "lucky" if a bullet ignited the gas tank and his airplane exploded in a ball of fire. If not, he burned alive slowly or leaped from the cockpit, hurtling toward a quick death on the ground. Commanders refused to issue parachutes, because they thought pilots would abandon their planes in a tight spot, rather than fight. Not having a parachute was supposed to make a pilot fight more bravely. So men died needlessly for lack of a few yards of silk cloth.

As the war continued, it became clear that men and weapons, by themselves, were not enough to achieve victory. "Oil is probably more important at this moment than anything else," said Walter Long, a friend of Churchill's. "You may have men, munitions, and money, but if you do not have oil . . . all your other advantages would be of . . . little value."[15] Long was right. Eventually, the side that won the race for oil would win the war. The goal, then, was not to win any single battle or campaign. It was to protect and expand one's own oil supplies while depriving the enemy of fuel.

With their battleships trapped in port by the British fleet, the Germans turned to the U-boat (for *Unterseeboot*, or "undersea boat"), or submarine. Undersea raiders, however, needed two sources of power. When underwater, they ran on electrical batteries. Yet battery power did not last long. Every day, the submarine had to surface and move for several hours on its gasoline or diesel (oil) engine to recharge its batteries. Naturally, surfacing exposed the submarine to attack by ships and airplanes patrolling near enemy coasts. Even so, the stealthy, silent raider was a potent weapon.

The Germans turned their submarines against Allied ships. Their favorite targets were not warships, which could destroy a surfaced U-boat with gunfire or a submerged one with depth charges, bombs timed to explode underwater. Instead, U-boats attacked merchant ships, preferably oil tankers. Although Americans favored the Allies, they stayed neutral for most of the war, wanting to trade rather than fight. However, U-boats began sinking American ships bound for Britain; Standard Oil alone lost six tankers carrying oil to Britain. The U.S. Congress replied by declaring war on Germany in April 1917. As the Royal Navy tightened its grip on the sea-lanes, a million American troops crossed the pond, as they called the Atlantic Ocean.

So did American oil. While Persian oil fueled the Royal Navy, it was not nearly enough to supply the growing numbers of Allied trucks, tanks, and airplanes. In 1917, severe oil shortages threatened to paralyze the British and French armies. America came to the rescue. For the last year of the war, its oil and gasoline met 80 percent of the Allies' needs.

As the Allies got more fuel, Germany got less. Allied warships

48

German U-Boat Sinks an English Cargo Ship, painting by Adolf Bock, 1941.

49

blockading German ports cut off supplies of food, raw materials, and fuel from South America and the Dutch East Indies. With its oil reserves fast running out, Germany found it harder and harder to meet its needs. As a result, machinery in war factories that ran on oil ground to a halt, or wore out for lack of lubricating oil. Fuel shortages limited military operations. Hundreds of fighter planes sat on runways without fuel, targets for Allied pilots. Submarines could not put to sea.

Germany gave up on November 11, 1918. Those who knew the whole story of the war understood that the Germans lost not only because the Allies had more soldiers and better weapons, but from a deeper cause. Oil alone did not bring victory, but victory would have been impossible without the black stuff. Ten days after the German surrender, Lord Curzon, a high British official, declared: "The Allied cause had floated to victory upon a wave of oil."[16]

By the fall of 1918, it was clear that a nation's prosperity, even its very survival, depended on securing a safe, abundant supply of cheap oil. Few had imagined that this could be possible when World War I began.

IV

AUTOMOBILES AND MIDDLE EASTERN OIL

It's always been about oil when it comes to the Middle East. From the borders drawn by the British and French after the Great War to the current flare-up in Iraq, the simple fact is that not one drop of western blood would have ever been shed were it not for Persian Gulf crude.

—Sean Finnegan
CEO, Geomentum, a media company

Metal Demons for the Masses

Although oil played a critical part in World War I, it began to change the world in a major way only after the guns fell silent. This was because the automobile revolutionized transportation.

The auto's demand for gasoline saved John D. Rockefeller's fortune when electric lighting replaced kerosene lamps. Yet that was just the beginning. We get a hint of the coming change from a conversation an American overheard during a visit to Paris a decade before the war. In an emotional outburst, a man damned the automobile as a frightful thing, a devil's toy. "Within only two or three years, every one of you will . . . be the boastful owner of a metal demon." Then he warned that "the quiet of the world is ending forever."[1] He was right. The automobile has changed the way people live, and thus the course of history.

In the late 1800s, Europeans set out to invent a vehicle that could move on its own; that is what "automobile" means. Inventors agreed that, to work, it should have four wheels, a starter, brakes, a steering device, and seats for passengers. Above all, it needed a power source to make it move.

Various power sources were tried. Like any other steam engine, the steam automobile had a boiler that produced steam to turn the wheels. But instead of coal, the boiler ran on oil, as did the boilers of battleships. Invented by identical twin brothers Francis E. and Freelan O. Stanley, the Stanley Steamer, an American model, could travel at an astounding 127 miles an hour on flat ground. The Steamer's only drawbacks were high cost and a record of deadly boiler explosions.

51

Electric cars never exploded. Quiet and easy to control, they ran on a battery, reaching speeds of up to eighty miles an hour. Unfortunately, there were few places to recharge the battery, which was also expensive and heavy and wore out quickly. Electric cars were set aside, though they would make a comeback in the early years of the twenty-first century.

Gasoline became the preferred fuel. Easy to make, it took up little

The Stanley Steamer could travel up to 127 miles per hour. (c. 1903)

space and produced strong bursts of energy. Perfected in Germany in the 1890s, the gasoline-fueled internal combustion engine soon caught on in the United States. Yet, as in Europe, an auto was a luxury for the wealthy. Craftsmen built autos one at a time, with all the experts at a single workstation. Workers swarmed around a vehicle, each applying his special skills. It took twelve to fourteen hours for a team to build a single auto. As a result, companies made only a few prize vehicles each year. For example, the Pierce-Arrow, an American model, cost $3,700, a fortune back then. (What cost $3,700 in 1913 would cost $83,577 in 2011.)

52

Henry Ford's introduction of assembly-line production revolutionized manufacturing and created millions of jobs. (c. 1919)

Henry Ford changed the way we build autos, and much else besides. A Michigan farm boy with a passion for machinery, Ford became the father of mass production. His goal, he said, was to put an automobile within reach of everyone who held a job. So, instead of having workers gather around the vehicle they were building, Ford brought the vehicle to workers posted along an assembly line. Since an auto has thousands of parts, he broke each task into a series of smaller ones. "The man who places a part doesn't fasten it," he explained. "The man who puts in a bolt does not put on the nut; the man who puts on the nut does not tighten it."[2]

An auto grew as it moved along the assembly line on a conveyor belt. The belt paused briefly at each workstation, allowing a worker, or group of workers, to do a single, simple task. Each vehicle was an exact copy of any other, down to its color—black. "The way to make automobiles," said Ford, "is to make one automobile just like another automobile, to make them all alike . . . just like one pin is like another pin when it comes from a pin factory, or one match is like another match when it comes from the match factory."[3]

Ford's assembly-line method cut production time to ninety-three minutes per vehicle. Shorter production time increased the number of autos and reduced their cost. By 1928, a mass-produced Ford Model T sold for $295, a price nearly everyone could afford. Sturdy and reliable, Ford's Tin Lizzie went twenty-five miles on a gallon of gasoline, more than most of today's sport-utility vehicles (SUVs). Thanks to Ford and fellow automakers, especially the General Motors Corporation, the number of autos in the United States grew from 1.8 million in 1914 to 27 million in 1929—that is, one for every five people. When European companies adopted Ford's assembly-line method, their sales soared, too. (In 2007, there were over 255 million registered motor vehicles in the United States, or one vehicle for every 1.1 people.)

Besides creating millions of jobs, the auto industry provided a public service, particularly in cities. Nowadays we think of the auto,

53

Using Henry Ford's assembly line, workers could put a car together in just ninety-three minutes. (c. 1910s)

correctly, as a major source of air pollution. Yet a century ago, people did not see it that way at all. Instead, they praised it as cleaner, healthier, and safer than the most common means of transportation, the horse. American and European cities usually had one horse to every four people. Horses pulled buggies, carriages, cabs, wagons, fire engines, and streetcars, called buses. Most homes had a public stable nearby, or one in the backyard, if the family could afford to own a horse.

But horses were dangerous. Runaway animals trampled pedestrians to death. The constant clatter of iron horseshoes on cobblestoned streets rattled people's nerves and even drove some out of their minds. Worse, horses were the chief cause of pollution in cities, for you cannot toilet train a horse. It will relieve itself when it must, wherever it pleases. A horse produces up to thirty-five pounds of manure and a quart of urine a day. These wastes affected people's health and quality of life for the worse.

54

In 1900, for example, New York City had about 175,000 horses. These left an estimated six million pounds of fresh manure and nearly

A horse that died in the street was heavy, so it was left to decay until it was light enough to be moved. (c. 1890)

44,000 gallons of urine in the streets each day. Sanitation workers patrolled the streets in wagons (horse-drawn), armed with rakes and shovels. Unable to bury the waste fast enough in landfills, they piled manure in vacant lots across the city. Often manure piles rose to a height of forty, even fifty, feet. Experts predicted that if the situation was left unchecked, manure piles would reach third-story windows within thirty years! Horses also died in the streets from age, abuse, and overwork. Since a dead horse was heavy (about 1,300 pounds) and difficult to move, sanitation workers left it to rot away, then carted off the bones. For example, in 1880, an average year, workers removed some 15,000 horse carcasses.[4]

The smell of horse manure could be overpowering. It penetrated houses; diners in luxury restaurants complained of their food's "horsey" taste. Rain turned streets into rivers of liquefied manure. Manure blocked sewers, which overflowed onto sidewalks. Fashionable ladies in long dresses had to wade through the sticky goo or hire a "crossing sweeper" for a few pennies to clear a path.

Spring and summer were the worst seasons. Warm weather brought flies; in the 1890s an estimated three billion of them bred each day in horse manure in New York City. Manure piles, alive with wriggling white maggots, seemed to move on their own. Adult flies carried bacteria that caused food poisoning, diarrhea, tetanus, and typhoid. Dry weather turned manure into brown dust, fine as talcum powder. Wind blew the dust onto people's food and into their eyes, noses, and mouths. New York's health department blamed this "street dust" for 20,000 deaths in the city each year.[5]

So people turned to the auto not only for its convenience but as a lifesaver. It represented life, health, quiet, and fresh air. In 1899, *Scientific American* magazine explained:

> The improvement in city living conditions by the general adoption of the motorcar can hardly be overestimated. Streets clean, dustless and odorless, with lighter rubber tired vehicles moving swiftly and noiselessly over their smooth expanse, would eliminate a greater part of the nervousness, distraction, and strain of modern metropolitan life.[6]

55

City dwellers treated gasoline exhaust fumes as a minor nuisance compared to the horrors of horse manure. As autos replaced horses, some could barely contain their joy at the change. God bless gasoline! One writer praised it in flowery words, calling it "the juice of the fountain of eternal youth. . . . It is health. It is comfort."[7] Of course, the soaring number of motor vehicles in the United States and Europe demanded ever more of this marvelous "juice." Where would it come from? Who would control it? Who would profit from it?

The Scramble for Middle Eastern Oil

By the 1920s, newly discovered oil fields in Mexico and Venezuela went into production. In North America, oil companies struck it rich in Canada, Oklahoma, and California. In 1930, a wildcatter named Columbus Marion "Dad" Joiner found oil in the sandy hills of east-central Texas. Dubbed the Black Giant, this field made America the world's top producer for a generation. In all, the Black Giant's 30,340 wells drained 5.2 billion barrels of oil from Texas reservoir rock.

Europeans, as ever, wanted to keep this vital natural resource under their own control. While Iranian production soared under the British, it could not satisfy Europe's thirst for oil. Surely, geologists believed, the Middle East held other fields at least as productive as Iran's. European science, industry, and government saw the need to work together. The scientist's job was to find new oil fields. The businessman's job was to extract the black gold and bring it to market at a profit. The politician's and soldier's job was to create opportunities for the others, then protect their investments by armed force.

British leaders had made control of Middle Eastern oil a major war aim. Even as World War I raged in Europe, the government in London looked to the future—to Mesopotamia. Turkey had ruled the Land of the Two Rivers for nearly four centuries. Since the 1520s, it had divided the area into three provinces, each taking its name from its chief city: Basra, Baghdad, Mosul. It ruled with an iron fist. Anyone who dared resist Turkish domination, or even criticize it, was jailed, tortured, or killed.

After seizing Basra to protect the refineries at Abadan, British

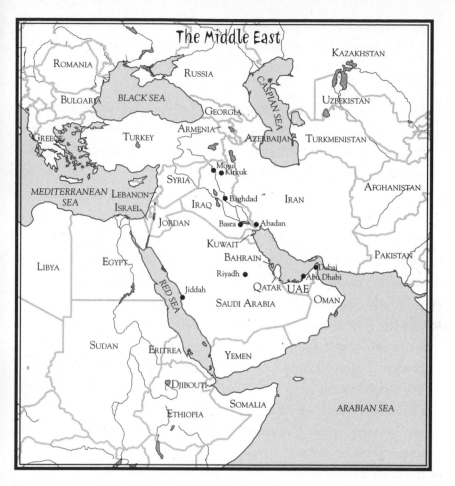

The Middle East

57

forces overran all of Mesopotamia. When they captured Baghdad, its citizens went wild with joy. Happy Baghdadis toppled statues of Turkish sultans, or emperors. Crowds lined the streets, cheering and tossing handfuls of candy to their liberators, a symbol of welcome and respect.

General Sir Stanley Maude, the British commander, had posters in English and Arabic put up throughout Baghdad. They said:

> Our armies do not come into your cities and lands as conquerors
> or enemies, but as liberators. . . . [Your citizens] have been subject
> to the tyranny of strangers [the Turks] . . . and your forefathers
> and yourselves have groaned in bondage. . . . But you people of
> Baghdad . . . are not to understand that it is the wish of the
> British Government to impose upon you alien institutions. . . .

It is the hope and desire of the British people . . . that the Arab race may rise once more to greatness and renown among the peoples of the earth.[8]

These were fine words but empty ones. For while the general promised liberty in the name of his government, and may even have meant it, British leaders had other plans. They had already decided that if Mesopotamia had oil, Britain must have it, whatever the people might wish.

In 1919, a conference met in Paris to work out peace treaties with the defeated nations and create a world organization, the League of Nations, to prevent future wars. Britain and France had a major say in the league's affairs; America refused to join, because President Woodrow Wilson and the Senate disagreed on what powers the league should have.

58

With America out of the picture, British and French diplomats had the league create a system of mandates for the Middle Eastern territories seized from Turkey. Under a mandate, a so-called advanced country (code for Britain or France) would govern a supposedly "backward" territory while helping it along the road to independence. But when it would be ready for independence was anybody's guess. For, in reality, mandates gave legal cover to foreign domination. France got the mandate for two former Turkish territories: Syria and Lebanon. Britain got the mandate for Palestine, Transjordan (now Jordan), and Mesopotamia. If oil was found in Mesopotamia, Britain promised to share some of it with France.

No sooner did Britain get

Prime Minister David Lloyd George insisted that Britain continue pursuing oil in Iraq in spite of the danger to soldiers. (c. 1919)

the mandate than it changed the name of Mesopotamia to Iraq. In Arabic, *Iraq* means "well-founded country." By changing the name, British officials wanted to give the impression that they ruled a unified nation. Yet changing a name is different from changing a reality.

Iraq was surely not well founded. Iraq was an artificial country. The Turks had never ruled it as a single, unified nation, but as three separate provinces—Basra, Baghdad, and Mosul—each with its own governor, police force, laws, courts, and tax system. Within each province, city folk resented the desert tribes, or Bedouins, and called them backward, thieving "sand people." Bedouins called city dwellers the "soft-handed ones," unmanly cowards corrupted by easy living. Throughout history, their warriors had raided the settled lands bordering the desert. Bedouins had always owed their loyalty to their families and tribes, not to any central government. Moreover, age-old hatreds between Sunni and Shia (both Muslim religious groups) and the Muslim but non-Arab Kurds might easily erupt into civil war.

The one thing that united Iraqis was their hatred of the mandate. A proud people, their ancestors had once led the world in the sciences and arts. While the British called themselves liberators, Iraqis rightly felt that they had merely replaced the Turks as foreign masters. The British quickly took over Iraq, ruling it in their own interests, not those of its people.

Iraqi resentment boiled over in the spring of 1920. Muslim religious leaders declared jihad, or holy war, against the infidel occupiers. Anti-British demonstrations broke out in the chief cities: Baghdad, An Najaf, Tikrit, Karbala, Fallujah. American soldiers would later fight in these same places.

Across Iraq, city dwellers and tribesmen, Sunni and Shia, joined forces against the common enemy. Armed bands roamed the countryside, ambushing British patrols and blowing up railroad trains that brought supplies to their outposts. Extremists kidnapped British soldiers, tortured them, and then beheaded them to spread terror among their comrades. Many Britons, already sick of war, wanted to get out of Iraq immediately. Yet the government refused. Its reason: oil. Prime Minister David Lloyd George explained: "If we leave we may find a year or two after we departed that we have handed over to the French and Americans some of the richest oilfields in the world."[9] The prime minister felt in his bones that Iraq was a future oil bonanza.

When it came to terrorism, however, the British had lessons to teach Iraqis. Although greatly outnumbered, they had the advantage. British gunboats patrolled Iraq's rivers, shelling villages for any reason, or for no reason at all. Groups of British armored cars and trucks, called flying columns, set out in all directions. When they reached a village suspected of sheltering rebels, the vehicles' machine guns would cover the troops as they sprang from their trucks. Moving quickly, the troops burned crops with flamethrowers, tossed dynamite into water wells, and blew up houses, making families homeless.

The worst threat came on wings. British airplanes met no opposition, for the rebels had no aircraft. Pilots ranged across Iraqi skies at will, bombing and machine-gunning suspected rebel villages. Unable to tell women and children from rebels as they sped by, pilots killed both innocents and fighters. Iraqis, a British airman boasted, "now know what real bombing means, in casualties and damage; they now know that within 45 minutes a full-sized village can be practically wiped out and a third of its inhabitants killed or injured by four or five machines which offer them . . . no effective means of escape."[10] That officer, Major Arthur Harris, would lead Britain's air offensive against Germany during World War II. Nicknamed "Bomber" Harris, he would apply the lessons learned in Iraq on a much wider, and deadlier, scale.

It took seven months to smash the rebellion, at a cost of 450 British and perhaps 10,000 Iraqi lives. Iraqis never forgot, or forgave, what the British did in 1920. Years later the dictator Saddam Hussein would constantly remind them of it.

The rebellion also taught the British a political lesson. To keep the country calm, they needed to set up a government Iraqis could accept, but one led by a stooge who owed them everything. "What we want," an official said bluntly, is a ruler "we can safely leave while pulling the strings ourselves."[11] To play that part, they chose Faisal ibn Hussein al Hashem, an Arabian prince descended from the Prophet Muhammad, the founder of Islam. (*Faisal* means "the sword flashing down at a stroke" in Arabic.) In 1921, Faisal was invited to be king of Iraq. After accepting the invitation, he won popular approval in an election rigged by British officials; British military police arrested critics. In return, His Majesty signed a treaty of friendship, giving British "advisers" control of his country's affairs, including oil exploration. Ordinary Iraqis considered Faisal a traitor who had betrayed them to greedy foreigners.

Where to look for the black stuff? The most obvious place was Baba Gurgur, near the northern city of Kirkuk, in Mosul Province. There the king of Babylon, Nebuchadnezzar, had thrown Jews into a "fiery furnace" that still raged, and oil seeps dotted the countryside. In October 1927, six years after Faisal came to the throne, Britain's dream of Iraqi oil came true. After drilling to a depth of 1,500 feet, the bit bored into reservoir rock. Suddenly a gusher burst from the ground, followed by a cloud of natural gas that blotted out the sun for several minutes. Two drillers died in the eruption. Oil flowed at a rate of 95,000 barrels a day until work crews brought the well under control nine days later. Overnight Kirkuk became the largest oil discovery in the world so far, earning the title Capital of Black Gold.[12]

Yet the most productive oil fields lay undiscovered not in Iran or Iraq but to the south, in the Persian Gulf and Arabian Peninsula. Called Arabia for short, the peninsula, an area about the size of Texas, has the largest oil reserves on the planet. Many have died to win and hold Arabian oil, and many more will likely do so in the future.

Onward to the Persian Gulf!

The 1930s were good years for Middle Eastern oil exploration. After the discovery at Baba Gurgur, attention shifted to Bahrain, a small island (413 square miles) in the Persian Gulf. Major Frank Holmes, a mining engineer, had served with the British army fighting the Turks during World War I. The Middle East fascinated him, its people and landscape so different from anything he had known. After the war, Holmes retired from the army. For several years he wandered from

61

place to place, running small businesses, none successfully, while learning Arabic and Arab ways. When Holmes reached Bahrain, he noticed oil seeps in various places. Yet when he suggested drilling for oil, the island's ruler, Sheik Hamad al-Khalifa, said Bahrain needed water more than oil. Holmes took up the challenge, using his engineering skills to drill water wells. The grateful sheik rewarded him with an oil concession.

62

An Indian Army guard protecting the Kirkuk oil fields in Iraq. (1945)

Drilling for oil is expensive, and Holmes could not afford to do it on his own. When he went to London to raise money, businessmen turned him down. Oil on a desert island! Why, my dear sir, the very idea is fantasy, a lunatic's dream! So Holmes packed his bags and sailed for America. Only one company, Gulf Oil, showed interest in his idea. Gulf Oil had been born at Spindletop, and Texans were risk takers.

In October 1931, drilling began at Jabal Dukhan (Mountain of Smoke), near an oil seep. *Jabal* is Arabic for "hill surrounded by flat country"—that is, a possible dome above a layer of reservoir rock. Seven months later, Holmes's drillers brought in the first gusher. From then on, the people of Bahrain called Holmes Abu Naft (Father of Oil).

Though rich, the Bahrain field was no "elephant," drillers' slang for a supergiant oil field. However, the elephant of all elephants slept just twelve miles west of Bahrain, beneath the Arabian Desert.

The Oil World of Ibn Saud

The Arabian Peninsula is almost entirely desert. Sand mountains heaped up by the wind occupy much of its interior. Bedouins move constantly across the desert, searching for water and pasture for their herds of camels, sheep, and goats. These nomads get practically all they need from their animals: meat, milk, cloth of woven hair. They get weapons, cooking gear, and other manufactured goods by trading meat and milk with the people who live in oases. An oasis is a fertile desert area, thanks to rain and snow that falls in distant mountains. Slowly rainwater and melted snow soak into the ground. Over centuries the water filters downhill, through layers of porous rocks, and eventually returns to the surface as springs or is dug out as wells. These supply the water for date trees and the grain crops that oasis people grow in their fields. Several oasis cities border the peninsula's west coast, along the Red Sea. Among these are Mecca and Medina, the birthplaces of Islam in the seventh century.

The Arabian Peninsula holds the world's richest oil fields. It also has the only country named for a family: the al Saud. That country, Saudi Arabia, is the creation of a giant in modern Middle Eastern

63

history. Westerners called him Ibn Saud, a shortened version of his full
name—Abdul Azis bin Abdul Rahman bin Faisal al Saud.

Ibn Saud (1880–1953) was an impressive man. Tall and lean,
with gleaming white teeth and dark eyes, he stood head and shoulders
above most Arabs. Gertrude Bell, a British official, painted this word
picture of him:

> He is a man of splendid physique, standing well over six
> feet, and carrying himself with the air of one accustomed
> to command. . . . [He has] full-fleshed nostrils, prominent
> lips and long, narrow chin, accentuated by a pointed beard.
> His hands are fine, with slender fingers. . . . His deliberate
> movements, his slow, sweet smile, and the contemplative
> glance of his heavy-lidded eyes . . . add to his dignity and
> charm. . . . Nevertheless, report credits him with powers of
> physical endurance rare even in hard-bitten Arabia. Among

64

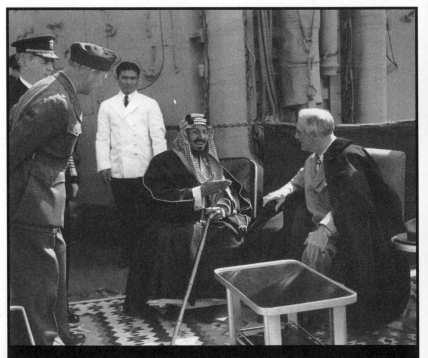

Ibn Saud (seated, left) with President Franklin D. Roosevelt.
(February 14, 1945)

men bred to the camel saddle, he is said to have few rivals as a tireless rider. . . . He combines with his qualities as a soldier that grasp of statecraft which is yet more highly prized by the tribesmen.[13]

He was, then, a shrewd man who could be hard as nails if need be.

Ibn Saud was born into a noble family in a land torn by tribal warfare. When Ibn Saud was ten, his family, the al Saud, suffered a stunning defeat at the hands of a rival family. To avoid vengeance later, the victors usually killed the losers' sons, whatever their age. Ibn Saud escaped by hiding in a leather bag hung from a camel saddle. He fled to Kuwait, a tiny country located on the Persian Gulf, between the Arabian Peninsula to the south and Iraq to the north and east. *Kuwait* means "fortress built on the water," and it was exactly that for the youngster and other al Saud survivors. Kuwait's emir (ruler) gave them shelter. In 1901, at the age of twenty-one, Ibn Saud took his revenge. With only twenty men, half of them slaves, he returned to Arabia to reclaim his family's lands with the help of the Wahhabis.

Wahhabi means "followers of Wahhab." Muhammad ibn Abd al-Wahhab was an eighteenth-century Muslim religious leader. Today we would call him a fundamentalist, a person who opposes anything that differs from the original or basic teachings of the Prophet Muhammad. In the 1760s, al-Wahhab set out to "cleanse" Arabia by returning it to the "pure" Islam originally taught by the Prophet around the year 620. Al-Wahhab believed that Allah (God) demanded total, unquestioning obedience to Islamic law—willingly if possible, by force if necessary. His followers, despising all luxury as sinful vanity, smashed decorated mosques (Muslim houses of worship); they also banned music and tobacco. Since the al Saud had always been deeply religious, they became friends and allies of al-Wahhab.[14]

Over a century later, Ibn Saud turned to the Wahhabis for help. Their warriors, called the Ikhwan—Arabic for "the Brotherhood"—flocked to his green banner. Stern Bedouin warriors, they wore robes of the whitest white and beards dyed the blackest black. The Brotherhood spared no one who lacked "holiness," as they defined it. "I have

65

seen them hurl themselves on their enemies," an Arab eyewitness wrote, "utterly fearless of death, not caring how many fall, advancing rank after rank with only one desire—the defeat and annihilation of the enemy. They normally [spare] neither boys nor old men, veritable angels of death from whose grasp no one escapes."[15]

By 1925, the Brotherhood had conquered almost the entire Arabian Peninsula for Ibn Saud. Apart from a few independent places, such as Yemen, Oman, and Qatar, Ibn Saud ruled the peninsula from the Persian Gulf to the Red Sea. He welded its tribes and towns, oases and Bedouin bands, into a nation. In 1932, he named it Saudi Arabia and declared himself king.

In creating a nation where none had ever existed, Ibn Saud took on a daunting task. For starters, he had to organize a government,

66

The Islamic fundamentalist Wahhabi warriors helped Ibn Saud conquer the Arabian Peninsula to establish the oil-rich nation of Saudi Arabia. (date unknown)

provide public services, and see to national defense. Furthermore, each year thousands of devout Muslims came on pilgrimage to Mecca and Medina from across the world. As "Keeper of the Holy Places," Ibn Saud had to care for their needs and safety. All that cost money, which he did not have. In the old fighting days, his "treasury" fit neatly into a few camel saddlebags. But those days were gone.

The king turned to an Englishman for advice. Harry St. John Philby was an Arabist, a person who studies Arabic language, literature, and history. Philby fell in love with everything Arab, spending much of his life studying, exploring, and writing about the Middle East. During his travels he visited Saudi Arabia and decided to make it his home. To support himself, Philby won the sole right to sell Ford automobiles in the country.[16]

When Philby met Ibn Saud, they became such good friends that he converted to Islam. The king gave him the name Abdullah, which means "slave of God," and a beautiful slave girl, Mariam, by whom he had two sons. Slavery had existed in the Middle East for thousands of years. Saudi Arabia abolished it in 1962. Ibn Saud had twenty-two wives and scores of official lovers, or concubines; his wives gave him about 100 children. His concubines gave him others, but we do not know how many.

One day, the king invited

Harry St. John Philby in Arab robes, from his 1922 book, *The Heart of Arabia, a Record of Travel and Exploration.* (date unknown)

67

Philby to take an automobile ride with him into the desert outside Riyadh, the capital. His Majesty was depressed and needed a time-out with good company. Philby knew about his friend's money troubles. Yet, he said, everyone he met seemed "like folk asleep on buried treasure"—black gold. Saudi Arabia was so close to Bahrain, it had to rest atop the same oil-bearing rock formations. "Oh, Philby," Ibn Saud sighed, "if anyone offered enough money, I would give him all the concessions he wanted."[17]

When Philby approached European oil companies, they turned him away. Money was tight because the world was in the midst of a serious economic crisis: the Great Depression. Finally, early in 1933, Philby turned to Standard Oil of California (SoCal), a Rockefeller company. SoCal agreed to pay Ibn Saud $250,000, in gold, in return for a share of the profits for sixty years if it found oil.

68

Although they were not Muslim, Ibn Saud liked Americans. To begin with, they were not British; he distrusted the British, fearing they would do to his country what they had done to Iraq. The king also felt that he owed Americans a debt of gratitude. Christian missionaries had set up medical clinics in several Middle Eastern countries, but not in Saudi Arabia. Nevertheless, the king sent relatives for treatment at the American clinic in Kuwait. When he developed a serious eye infection, an American doctor cured him in a week, saving him from blindness.

The first SoCal explorers arrived from Bahrain by airplane in the winter of 1933. They came, Philby recalled, "from the skies on their flying carpets with strange devices for probing the bowels of the earth in search of the liquid muck for which the world clamors to keep its [greedy] machines alive." The Bedouins found them a strange lot. Mostly Texans and Oklahomans, these lanky men wore colorful cowboy boots, broad-brimmed Stetson hats, and blue denim work clothes. The Americans, for their part, had to adjust to sandstorms and 120-degree heat on a normal day. Bedouin food was "strange," to put it mildly. For example, Bedouins ate locusts as a delicacy and a source of protein. "They boil them, dry them in the sun, pound them in [a] mortar and make a sort of locust mush," a Texan wrote home. "I think I'll stick to oatmeal."[18]

After many disappointments, on March 4, 1938, drillers struck oil at Dammam, near the Persian Gulf, opposite Bahrain. A week earlier, American drillers had brought in Kuwait's first oil well. Yet Dammam, the first Arabian super-elephant, was the real treasure. By year's end, oil was flowing freely from the field, forced to the surface by natural pressure. A separate company called Aramco (Arabian American Oil Company) was formed and a pipeline built to al-Khobar, an oasis on the coast. From there, pumps would deliver it to American tankers anchored offshore. They still do.

The honor of opening the valve at al-Khobar went to Ibn Saud. On May 1, 1939, the king led 2,000 guests to the site in 500 Ford cars. After oil began to flow into the SoCal tanker *D. G. Schofield,* the royal party returned to Riyadh. On the ride back across the desert, to pass the time, "the king, along with some of his brothers and older sons, sang Bedouin raiding songs from their youth."[19]

The discovery of oil in the Arabian Peninsula would bring an era of plenty, but not just yet. Four months after Ibn Saud opened the valve at al-Khobar, World War II shut down nearly all production in the Persian Gulf region. In Kuwait, the foreign oil companies, acting on orders from their home governments, plugged the wells with cement in case they should fall into German hands. In Saudi Arabia, nearly all operations ceased, as most American workers left for home. Yet, as in World War I, oil would become what a French politician called "the blood of victory."[20]

V

HOPELESS MONSTERS

No matter how well fed, equipped or officered, without oil and gasoline the modern army is a hopeless monster, mired and marked for destruction.

—*T. H. Vail Motter*
U.S. Army historian

Adolf Hitler's War for Vengeance and Oil

World War II was the most destructive conflict in history. Although we will never know the exact number, historians believe the war (1939–1945) claimed the lives of seventeen million fighters. In addition, no fewer than forty million civilians died as a result of air raids, massacres, starvation, disease, and other war-related causes. The lives disrupted and the property wrecked by the war are beyond calculation.

As in the previous war, oil took center stage, only more so. In certain ways, black gold helped cause World War II, then governed its course and decided its outcome. Oil did not guarantee victory then, any more than it had done before. But all the generals and political leaders thought about oil always. They had to, because victory would have been impossible for the side that did not have enough oil or failed to deny it to the enemy.

Abraham Lincoln said, "The past is the cause of the present, and the present will be the cause of the future."[1] World War II grew out of the earlier conflict. Allied leaders had used the slogan "the war to end all wars" to persuade their people to fight. They said the enemy was so evil that its defeat and punishment would finally abolish war, as medicine cures disease. Harsh peace treaties stripped the defeated of territory, including their overseas colonies, and forced them to pay for "crimes against peace" in hard cash. In doing so, the winners created bitter grievances among the losers, especially Germany, where many felt that only another war could restore their national pride and power. Among them was Adolf Hitler.

Hitler was at once a brilliant public speaker and a savage hater. The man had an uncanny gift for expressing the humiliation ordinary Germans felt but could not put into words themselves. After World War I he organized the National Socialist German Workers' Party, or Nazi Party. ("Nazi" is a shortening of the party's German name.) But Hitler did not want only to restore the Germans' national pride. A

71

Adolf Hitler was a self-taught expert on oil and read and spoke about it frequently. (c. April 28, 1939)

72

German soldiers riding through the wreckage during a blitzkrieg operation, which means "lightning war." (September 1939)

racist, he believed that nature had created certain peoples inferior to others. Germans, he claimed, were a master race, destined to extermi- nate their inferiors, chiefly the Jewish people. While most people saw war as evil, though sometimes necessary, Hitler thought it the highest good—"the father of all things." Hitler insisted, "He who wants to live should fight, therefore, and he who does not want to battle in this world of eternal struggle does not deserve to be alive."[2] In short, the Nazi leader knew no limits. He would commit any crime, invade any country, to conquer the world, killing whomever he wished and enslaving almost everyone else.

Secretly at first, then openly, Hitler rebuilt Germany's armed forces. The dictator had served during World War I as a common soldier. He remembered how German armies, millions of men, had gotten bogged down in the mud and blood of the trenches. Never again! He and his generals envisioned a new kind of warfare. Speed would be everything. Fast-moving forces must punch through the enemy, slip around him, and fly over him. They must use masses of tanks and aircraft to wage blitzkrieg. (*Blitzkrieg* is German for "lightning war.")

Oil was the lifeblood of blitzkrieg. "To fight, we must have oil for our [war] machine," Hitler said, correctly. A self-taught expert, he read and spoke about oil constantly. The weapons of blitzkrieg needed vast amounts of oil and gasoline. For example, the ME-109 fighter plane burned a hundred gallons of gasoline an hour. That was at cruising speed, not in a dogfight, where steep dives and sharp turns more than doubled the amount of fuel consumed. A panzer, or armored, division had 170 battle tanks. It also had hundreds of armored cars, motorized artillery, communications vehicles, field kitchens, mobile repair shops, and convoys of supply trucks and troop carriers. A German tank needed two gallons of fuel to travel one mile. A panzer division burned a thousand gallons of gasoline per mile on paved roads, twice that when charging across open fields. Where would all that fuel come from?[3]

World War I had answered this question for Hitler. The Allied blockade had taught him how dependent Germany was on imports of many raw materials, particularly oil. The dictator vowed to make Germany independent of outside sources. He began by stockpiling crude oil during his military buildup. Most of it came from the United States, Mexico, Venezuela, Romania, and a Soviet Russia ruled by Joseph Stalin, a dictator as brutal as Hitler himself. The Russian oil fields at Baku produced 170 million barrels a year. In return for Hitler's promise not to attack, Stalin sold him oil cheaply.

73

Most of Germany's oil, however, came from advances in technology made since World War I. Scientists learned that coal, if kept under great pressure and high temperature, liquefies into oil. Hitler built thirteen plants to make and refine synthetic (artificial) oil from coal, and Germany had plenty of coal in the Ruhr Valley. Synthetic oil was six times more expensive than natural oil to produce. However, cost meant nothing to Hitler, for he had to have oil not only to fuel his war machine but to supply Germany's war industries: weapons factories, shipyards, chemical plants. As with natural oil, refining synthetic oil also yielded nitrogen and methanol, ingredients in high explosives.

Hitler unleashed bliztkrieg on Poland at sunrise on September 1, 1939. World War II began with German forces bombing, blasting, breaking through, and rolling over Poland's defenders. Over the next eight months, the Germans conquered not only Poland but France, Holland, Belgium, Norway, and Denmark. Engineer units called oil commandos followed the advancing troops. Their mission: seize oil stockpiles before the retreating enemy destroyed them. While racing through France, for example, panzer divisions often refueled from enemy fuel depots. Only the English Channel halted the tanks' advance, preventing them from overrunning Britain.

Hitler knew he could not invade Britain unless he commanded the skies above it. To do that, he must first destroy the Royal Air Force (RAF). Here, however, the dictator faced an unexpected problem. While both sides had excellent airplanes and pilots, the RAF used a special blend of gasoline made only in the United States at that time. Called 100-octane fuel, it allowed aircraft engines to run more smoothly and gave more power than the 87-octane fuels used by all other air forces. (Automobiles ran on 40-octane fuel.) Thus, a first-line British fighter like the Spitfire could climb faster, fly higher, stay aloft longer, and turn more easily than any opponent. Although supposedly neutral, President Franklin D. Roosevelt favored Britain; no 100-octane gasoline ever reached Germany. Even so, Hitler had so many planes that it seemed he might destroy the RAF by sheer numbers. However, the RAF held the edge in combat, thanks to the gasoline it used. That edge helped decide who controlled the skies over Britain.

Unable to invade Britain, Hitler turned against Russia. Not only did he despise Russians as "racially inferior," he saw their oil as the key to his true goal of world conquest. His chief target was Baku. With these oil fields in his hands, he believed, nothing could stop him. "Germany will have all the means possible for waging war against continents," he boasted. "Nobody will be able to defeat her anymore."[4]

Hitler had ambitious plans. Once Baku was captured, he would send one army racing southward from there, across the Middle East to the lands of the oil-rich Persian Gulf. Meanwhile, another army, driving eastward across Russia, would link with the Japanese to conquer Asia. North and South America would then be "islands" surrounded by enemies fueled by unlimited supplies of oil. Britain, hopeless, would surrender without an invasion. Isolated, America would become Hitler's puppet—or so he imagined.

On June 22, 1941, two million German soldiers and 600,000 motorized vehicles invaded Russia under an umbrella of aircraft. Columns of supply trucks followed the ground forces stretching as far as the eye could see.

The Road to Pearl Harbor

Japan was a military dictatorship. Under Emperor Hirohito, the military ruled a nation of sixty million crowded into five mountainous islands lacking the raw materials needed by modern industry. These included rubber, iron, tin, copper, and oil—especially oil. Japan imported 80 percent of its oil from America. Like Britain, it wanted a supply it could control; otherwise foreigners might use oil as a weapon against it. For that reason, other Asian nations, underdeveloped but resource-rich, became tempting targets. In 1937, Japanese forces invaded China, then a huge but disunited country in the grip of a civil war. Japan's military was soon disappointed. An official report bluntly said that "there is no oil" in China.[5] There is in fact some, but it would not be found until the 1990s.

The Japanese military now looked south, toward the fields of the Shell Oil Company, a Dutch firm in the Dutch East Indies, today's nation of Indonesia. However, they feared that seizing these islands would lead to war with a European nation and its British and French allies. Their fears vanished when Hitler's blitzkrieg routed the Allies. In June 1941, Japanese forces invaded French Indochina, today the republics of Vietnam and Laos. Vietnam has wonderful deepwater harbors, ideal for naval bases from which to mount an invasion of the East Indies.

President Roosevelt watched these events with growing anxiety. Hitler had already overrun much of Europe. Now Japan threatened to do the same in Asia. Roosevelt decided to act before it was too late. A month after the invasion of Indochina, he halted the sale of oil and gasoline to Japan. The president's action forced Japan's leaders to choose between waging war with America and seeking peace on U.S. terms—that is, ending Japan's aggression in Asia. They chose war.

Time was against Japan. Its stockpile of oil would last two years at most. With each passing day, it would become harder for factories to make the goods civilians needed. Worse, the Japanese war machine would fall apart without oil. "If there were no supply of oil," an admiral noted, "battleships and any other warships would be nothing more than scarecrows," useless junk.[6]

The Japanese military decided to use Japan's dwindling stockpile in a desperate campaign for oil independence. Only the U.S. Pacific Fleet, based at Pearl Harbor in the Hawaiian Islands, stood in the aggressor's way. That fleet would be sunk in a surprise attack. The high command in Tokyo did not intend to invade Hawaii, let alone the U.S. mainland. Instead, while America struggled to recover from the blow, Japan would conquer the Philippine Islands, British Malaya (now part of Malaysia), and the Dutch East Indies in a series of bold, swift moves. These places had all the raw materials Japan needed. When America finally recovered, Japan would have grown too strong to defeat. Or so the military thought.

On December 7, 1941, a quiet Sunday morning, Japanese aircraft carriers launched their planes toward Pearl Harbor. In less than an hour, they sank or damaged eighteen warships, including eight battleships, and killed 2,323 American servicemen. Though a disaster for America, even this cloud had its silver lining.

The USS *Shaw* exploding in the Pearl Harbor attack. (December 7, 1941)

77

That Sunday the silver lining was black. When the attackers returned to their carriers, they knew they had not finished the job. Pearl Harbor had 4.5 million gallons of oil and gasoline stored in "tank farms," groups of huge storage tanks. Destroying these would have paralyzed American military operations in the Pacific for a year at least. Although his pilots wanted to attack again, Admiral Nagumo, the fleet commander, refused. Bad weather had caused his oil tankers to lag behind his battle fleet. Another attack, he reckoned, would probably use up the fleet's fuel, leaving it stranded at sea. Nagumo decided to play it safe. The admiral ordered his fleet to head for the tankers and then turn homeward after refueling. So, having gone to war for oil, Japan failed to deal the knockout blow for lack of oil at the critical moment.

Few Japanese noticed that the attack had not achieved its goal. Why should they? They were no longer alone, because Hitler declared war on America four days after Pearl Harbor. In the following weeks, Japanese forces rampaged across Asia. Fast-moving battle groups seized

Hong Kong, a British possession next to China, then Singapore, Britain's fortress city in Malaya. The Philippine Islands fell, as did the Dutch East Indies. The East Indies was a double prize. Japan gained not only its vast oil fields but the source of nearly all the world's natural rubber. No wonder the nation reveled in "victory fever." Schoolchildren stuck little Rising Sun flags into maps, marking each new conquest. Flag-waving adults sang and danced in the streets.

They should not have. Pearl Harbor united the American people as nothing had ever done. A war cry, "Remember Pearl Harbor," rang across the land. The tank farms the attackers missed would fuel American ships and aircraft out for revenge, but not until the American war effort had shifted into high gear.

America's Oil War at Home

President Roosevelt had begun to prepare for war after Hitler invaded Poland. Like it or not, he felt, America would become involved. Each month, thousands of men received draft notices, while the government spent billions on new weapons. To guarantee oil supplies, Roosevelt created the Petroleum Administration for War (PAW) six months before Pearl Harbor. The PAW enlisted oil-industry leaders to make sure everything ran smoothly. Meanwhile, the military made its plans, which all depended on oil. First, planners had to see that enough oil reached American forces and those of America's British and Russian allies. Second, they had to cripple the enemy's ability to wage war by attacking arms factories and oil supplies.

Hitler tried to torpedo their plans—literally. Within hours of declaring war, he ordered groups of submarines, called wolf packs, to attack shipping in American waters. "If we engage all our Gray Wolves along the American coast, we can bleed enemy shipping to death," said a German admiral.[7]

Hitler's wolf packs took the U.S. Navy by surprise. It had not ordered seaside cities to turn their lights off at night; apparently, nobody had thought of such a sensible move. As a result, vessels silhouetted against the shoreline from Maine to Florida became easy targets for enemy submarines. Merchant seamen went in fear of their lives. One recalled:

We was carrying fifty thousand barrels of Oklahoma crude and fifty thousand of high-test gasoline. It sure gives you a funny feeling. I thought we'd get it any minute. Man, those nights are killers! You sleep with your clothes on. Well, I don't exactly mean sleep. You lie there in bed with your clothes on. All of a sudden the old engines slow down and your heart speeds up. Someone knocks on the door and you rise right up in your bed and seem to lie there in the air. So it turns out it's only the watch. You settle down and try to light a cigarette if your hand don't shake too much. Not that you're scared of course. Oh nooooh![8]

Hundreds of cargo ships and scores of oil tankers "got it." People in coastal communities stared out to sea, horrified, as flames from burning ships lit the night sky. Submarine captains preferred tankers; the average tanker carried 130,000 barrels of oil. After several weeks of slaughter at sea, the U.S. Navy ordered a coastal blackout. Then it formed hunter-killer groups of aircraft and warships to sink U-boats. The tactic worked. As losses mounted, Hitler recalled the wolf packs to European waters. Although U-boats remained a danger throughout the war, what their crewmen called the "happy time" was over. Whenever they put to sea, they knew the odds were against their setting foot on dry land again.

Meanwhile, American oilmen coined a slogan: "You can't sink a pipeline." A pipeline, they

President Franklin D. Roosevelt created the Petroleum Administration for War to make sure American troops would not run out of oil. (c. December 27, 1933)

79

The Big Inch pipeline was built to carry oil from Texas to East Coast refineries with less vulnerability to attack. (c. 1942 or 1943)

80

said, could move oil across the country faster, more cheaply, and more safely than railroads or ships. Soon after Pearl Harbor, work began on the Big Inch pipeline. Completed in less than a year, it carried oil from Texas wells to eastern refineries, a distance of 1,400 miles. This engineering marvel crossed rivers, slung under the spans of bridges. It climbed the Allegheny Mountains, sometimes going nearly straight up. Each day, pumping stations, one every twenty-five miles, sent 300,000 barrels of crude through the pipeline. The Big Inch was so successful that another pipeline, the Little Big Inch ("Little" because it used narrower pipes) followed.

American refineries turned out five billion barrels of oil and gasoline during the war—that is, 70 percent of the fuel used by the Allies. Yet even this was not enough to meet all of America's civilian and military needs, plus those of its allies. The war effort came first. So the government limited the amount of gasoline a civilian could buy to four gallons a week, and reduced the highway speed limit to thirty-five miles per hour, since slower driving burns less fuel. These actions had important side benefits. Lower speeds caused the number of auto accidents to plummet, saving thousands of lives. To save fuel, workers formed car pools. Neighbors got to know each other better.

Joseph Stalin praised the American achievement. After the German invasion, he needed any help he could get, even if it came from the hated democracies. "This is a war of engines and octanes," the Russian dictator said at a banquet. "I drink to the American auto industry and the American oil industry."[9] Stalin gave credit where it was due. His forces could not have driven the invaders back without American aid. The Russian army received thousands of mass-produced Ford trucks. Though Hitler failed to take Baku, Russia lacked high-grade aviation fuel. America sent millions of gallons of its precious 100-octane gasoline. That fuel enabled Russia to master the skies over its own land, as it had helped the British. Still, the Allies could not win final victory without liberating occupied Europe and conquering Germany on its own soil.[10]

Victory in Europe

Hitler's forces would learn how it felt to be on the receiving end of blitzkrieg. The Allies planned to crush them in a giant vise. One jaw of the vise would close from the east, the other from the west. They would meet in the heart of Germany. While the Russians would move overland, American and British forces had to cross the English Channel, landing in Normandy on the French coast. From there they would advance across France, Belgium, and the Netherlands into Germany. Yet, just as Hitler could not invade Britain without crippling the RAF first, the Allies could not land in German-occupied France without crippling the German air force.

Stalin's beloved engines and octanes held the key to victory in the air war. Allied bombers were really four-engine "flying trucks" designed to carry heavy bomb loads. Slow-moving and hard to handle, they depended on fighters, nicknamed "little friends," for protection. To increase the fighters' range, Allied engineers gave them more powerful engines and drop tanks. These were extra gasoline tanks mounted under a fighter's wings that its pilot could drop when empty or before

American fighter planes were nicknamed "little friends" by Allied bombers. (c. 1944)

82

a dogfight. By escorting bombers to the target, fighters did two things. First, they forced German fighters to protect key targets like arms factories, railroads, and bridges rather than go on the attack. Second, the advantages of 100-octane gasoline allowed Allied fighters to shoot German fighters down in droves. In one week alone, in February 1944, the Americans lost 33 to the enemy's 692 fighters. No wonder pilots called it Big Week.

With the German air force collapsing, American and British bomber crews received an order: their chief aim was "to deny oil to enemy armed forces." Hundreds of bombers at a time visited Germany's synthetic-oil plants. After a raid, scout planes flew overhead every day to keep tabs on the progress of the repair crews. When the plant seemed ready to resume production, bombers struck again. The Germans knew the routine. "Today," workers would say, "we have finished rebuilding the plants and tomorrow the bombers will return."[11] Members of the repair crews were often slave laborers, men captured during Germany's blitzkrieg across Europe. Although they feared for their lives when

B-17 bombers striking oil refineries in Germany to halt oil production. (c. 1944)

83

the bombers came, they also knew that the raids hurt Hitler's forces, thus bringing the day of liberation closer.

The German war machine slowly fell apart. Although production of aircraft, tanks, and other weapons continued in underground factories, the army had to limit operations for lack of fuel. Less oil also meant fewer chemicals for explosives. Things became so bad that factories had to fill artillery shells with a mixture of explosives and rock salt, which reduced the force of the blast. That, in turn, saved the lives of countless Allied soldiers.

To fuel Allied forces when they landed in Normandy, on June 6, 1944, engineers built pipelines under the English Channel named for Walt Disney cartoon characters: Pluto, Dumbo, Bambi. The Germans fought desperately and well, but the Allied advantage in weapons and fuel forced them to retreat. Columns of 5,000-gallon tanker trucks fed by portable pipelines followed the pursuing tanks, covered by swarms of fighters. Sometimes Allied units advanced so quickly they outran their fuel supplies. "My men can eat their leather belts," growled

General George S. Patton, commander of the U.S. Third Army, "but my tanks have gotta have gas."[12]

At least Patton's tanks eventually got their gas. Enemy tanks seldom did. As the vise closed on Germany, crews used oxen to pull their tanks into position to save fuel for battle. But less fuel arrived each day. In one critical battle, the Germans massed 1,200 tanks at a river crossing to check the Russian advance. One by one, the tank engines sputtered as they ran out of fuel, until the Russians destroyed the entire force. On April 30, 1945, as Russian forces battled through the streets of Berlin, Hitler shot himself to escape capture. Guards poured a few precious gallons of gasoline, saved for the purpose, over the body and struck a match. It was a fitting end to the man who wanted oil to fuel his drive for world conquest.

84

An attack on a German oil refinery. (June 20, 1944)

America's War on Japanese Oil

As "victory fever" swept Japan after Pearl Harbor, America prepared for all-out warfare. Shipyards began turning out hundreds of warships of all kinds. While the navy got better battleships than ever before, these were no longer the fleet's heavy hitters. For any surface vessel, no matter how powerful, was prey to planes launched from aircraft carriers.

The aircraft carrier had many roles in World War II. It was (and is) a floating airfield that could reach any corner of the globe within days. Carrier-based planes could attack enemy ships and shore targets, and cover landing troops. Despite its great size, a carrier was very delicate. In fact, it was a thin-skinned bomb packed with fuel oil, aviation gasoline, and explosives. A well-placed bomb could turn the mightiest carrier into a flaming coffin within seconds.

In 1942, the navy organized fast-carrier "task forces" to fight the Japanese, thus coining a new term; a task force is a special unit designed for a special purpose. These units were miniature navies built around carriers. Since carriers were so delicate, a host of other vessels, including battleships, defended them with their guns. Battleships were no longer the queens of the fleet; their main job in World War

85

The USS *Enterprise* was the sixth aircraft carrier of the U.S. Navy and participated in more major action against Japan in World War II than any other U.S. ship. (c. April 12, 1939)

II was to bombard enemy shore defenses and protect the aircraft carriers. To reach the carriers, enemy planes would have to fly through a hailstorm of exploding shells and machine-gun bullets. Carriers defended themselves with fighters launched from their own decks. A fast-carrier task force could stay out of sight of land for months, thanks to its fleet trains. Each fleet train had groups of cargo ships and oilers that supplied a task force with everything it needed at sea.

86

Admiral Chester A. Nimitz, commander of U.S. naval operations in the Pacific, had a two-part plan for victory. The first part involved having fast-carrier task forces fight the Japanese navy and support attacks on enemy-held islands. Once marines and army troops secured an island, construction teams would improve its naval and air bases or build new ones. In fighting enemy ground troops, American forces would use oil-based weapons along with guns and explosives. Pilots would drop bombs filled with napalm. A mixture of gasoline and chemicals that made it thick and sticky, napalm covered a wide area, burning everything it touched. To destroy Japanese bunkers, fortified shelters built partly or entirely belowground, troops would use flame-throwing tanks. Like modern versions of Greek fire, these could send blazing streams of gasoline as far as 180 feet.

Admiral Chester A. Nimitz, the commander of U.S. naval operations in the Pacific. (c. 1943)

Each captured island would become a launchpad for attacking other islands. Nimitz did not want to take every Japanese-held island. Instead, after seizing a key island, his forces would "leapfrog" the others, simply passing them by. Cut off from Japan by thousands of miles of ocean, enemy troops could not halt the American advance. The goal of that advance was to capture islands close enough for heavy bombers to reach the Japanese homeland.

The second part of Nimitz's plan was to cut Japan's oil lifeline. Although carrier-launched dive-bombers would play a role, the main job fell to the submarines based at Pearl Harbor. Apart from fighting enemy warships, their top priority was sinking tankers carrying oil from the Dutch East Indies to Japan. As the fast-carrier task forces attacked islands, the undersea raiders sank enemy cargo ships. Things became so bad, a Japanese captain said, "that we were fairly certain a tanker would be sunk shortly after departing from port."[13]

Since it had counted on getting foreign oil, the Japanese government had not made a serious effort to develop synthetic oil. By early 1945, however, not one drop of oil reached Japan. As a result, factories closed and civilians had to get around on bicycles or on foot. People cooked their food and heated their homes by emptying libraries and burning books. Many built fires with charred beams salvaged from ruined buildings. There were plenty of those. Fleets of B-29 Superfortress bombers flew from island bases 1,500 miles away to blast Japan's cities with high explosives and incendiary bombs. For example, a raid on the night of March 9, 1945, killed over 84,000 people and burned sixteen square miles of central Tokyo. Never, in the entire history of war, had so many lost their lives in so short a time.

The Japanese military had managed to hoard about 200,000 barrels of oil and gasoline. This was a tiny amount, a drop in the bucket, since the fleet burned 2,900 barrels of oil an hour just cruising normally. The high command decided to give much of the fuel to the kamikaze (pronounced kah-mih-KAH-zee), or Divine Wind Special Attack Corps. This was a flowery name for volunteer units sent on one-way missions. Kamikaze pilots would crash their planes into American warships, especially aircraft carriers.

Suicide attacks made military sense to commanders, since they made the best use of Japan's last fuel reserves. A Japanese airman explained that suicide attacks would be more effective than ordinary

Teenage kamikaze pilots of the 72nd Shinbu Squadron the day before their mission. (c. May 26, 1945)

88

methods "because the power of the impact of the plane added to that of the bomb. Besides which the exploded gasoline caused fires. . . . Suicide attack was the only sure and reliable attack by airmen whose training had been limited because of the shortage of fuel."[14]

The high command hoped to make suicide attacks so costly that the Americans would not dare to invade Japan itself. In April 1945 over a thousand kamikazes defended Okinawa, an island just 350 miles south of Japan, chosen as the jump-off point for the planned invasion. Suicide pilots sank twenty-one American warships and damaged sixty-six others, but sank no aircraft carriers. The most famous kamikaze was not a plane at all, but the 64,000-ton *Yamato* (*Japan*), the largest battleship ever built. When the *Yamato* put to sea, it had just enough fuel to reach Okinawa. Its mission: destroy American troop transports at Okinawa and die honorably, with guns blazing. It did neither. American carriers launched swarms of dive-bombers and torpedo planes. The *Yamato* blew up and sank with nearly its entire crew. Its guns had not even scratched a troop transport.

Despite ever-increasing losses, Japan's warlords refused to admit defeat. Better that the nation die fighting than suffer the disgrace of surrender, they said. For that reason, they mobilized the civilian population to resist the Americans by any means, whatever the cost. Those without guns—millions of men, women, and children—were to charge the invaders with clubs and bamboo spears. Thus, the war's greatest tragedy still lay ahead, if the invasion took place as planned. Millions of people, Japanese and American, would certainly have died.

Yet that did not happen because of the atomic bomb. Secretly invented by American scientists, it made the invasion unnecessary. On August 6, 1945, an atomic bomb burst over the city of Hiroshima,

89

A panoramic view of Hiroshima after the atomic bomb exploded.

The atomic bomb exploding over Nagasaki. (August 9, 1945)

90

killing 68,000 people outright and injuring another 37,000, many of whom later died of radiation poisoning; 10,000 were declared missing, probably because they had been vaporized by the explosion. On August 9, a second atomic bomb destroyed Nagasaki, killing at least 35,000. Rather than face national suicide, Emperor Hirohito decided to end the war immediately. He ordered his armed forces to surrender.

World War II taught a brutal lesson. After occupation troops landed, an American naval officer interviewed former Japanese commanders. "What I learned then," he recalled, "was never lose a war, and the way to lose a war is to run out of oil."[15]

VI
RICHEST PRIZE,
GREATEST PROBLEM

[Middle Eastern oil is] one of the greatest material prizes
in world history—probably the richest economic
prize in the world.
—U.S. State Department memo, c. 1946

Oil is the greatest problem of all time—the greatest
polluter and promoter of terror. We should get rid of it.
—Shimon Peres
President of Israel

Miracles of Modern Chemistry

The end of World War II opened fresh opportunities for the oil industry. Large areas of Europe and Asia lay in ruins, and rebuilding required fleets of trucks and earthmovers. The end of rationing in America sent people on a spending spree. Overnight, Americans demanded new cars, homes, dishwashers, refrigerators—new everything. Recovery and progress needed oil to make, move, and run the things people wanted. Much of that oil would come from the Middle East. By the late 1940s, the region's existing oil fields had finally begun full-scale production, along with newly discovered fields. In 1948, the world's largest oil field was discovered at Ghawar, Saudi Arabia. Geologists believe the Ghawar field holds over eighty billion barrels of oil.

Middle Eastern oil, abundant and cheap, brought major changes in the way people lived. Thanks to it, coal, though still widely used in Europe to power factories and heat homes, steadily lost ground. That was good. For oil not only yields more energy than coal but is safer.

Horses were not the only danger to health in cities. Ever since the Industrial Revolution began in the 1700s, city dwellers had complained of the smoke from coal-burning factories. Coal smoke blackened the walls of their buildings and got into their lungs. At times it acted like poison gas. London, for example, was famous for its fog. Often fog settled over the city like a thick blanket, preventing you from seeing your hand in front of your face. Under certain weather conditions, coal smoke and humidity combined to create smog and droplets of sulfuric acid. Smog got into eyes, throats, and lungs. Smog killed. In December 1952, for example, 4,300 Londoners died in a week because of severe smog. As a result, the authorities banned coal and ordered a changeover to oil.

Around the time of London's Big Smoke, an American chemical company coined the slogan "Better things for better living through chemistry." A flood of useful products made from petrochemicals—chemicals derived from petroleum or natural gas—poured out of laboratories. Today about 6,000 products are made entirely of petrochemicals, or of petrochemicals blended with other materials. These products have become so common that we regard them as necessities. We take them for granted, not realizing where they come from.

Plastics head the list. The word comes from the Greek *plastikos*, meaning "able to be molded." Plastics take countless forms. In the early 1940s, when the first types appeared, *Popular Mechanics* magazine predicted that one day Americans would be "clothed in plastics from head to foot . . . live in a plastics house, drive a plastics auto and fly in a plastics airplane."[1] The prediction has not come true—yet. However, plastics have changed daily life by replacing natural materials such as wood, stone, metal, wool, and cotton. Though we do not live in all-plastic houses, many household goods begin as oil. And from plastic tubing to medicines, oil-based products protect our health.

Oil has made it possible for millions to eat regularly. Albert Bartlett of the University of Colorado defines modern agriculture as "the use of land to convert petroleum into food." Oil and gasoline do more than power farm machinery. Refineries produce ingredients for pesticides that kill crop-eating insects and for weed-killing herbicides. Most important, they produce nitrogen-rich ammonia, the basic ingredient in chemical fertilizers. Feeding an average family of four in America and Europe requires 930 gallons of petroleum a year.[2]

During the 1950s chemical fertilizers sparked the green revolution in food production. Each year millions of people who would have starved, or not been born at all, live. The green revolution led to the population explosion. From 1950 to 1990, world population nearly doubled, rising from 2.55 billion to 5.3 billion, thanks to increased food production. By 2030, experts expect world population to reach 8.2 billion. Thus, our lifestyle, even our daily bread, depends on black gold.

SOME PRODUCTS MADE FROM PETROLEUM

Health and Sanitary Products

Anesthetics
Antihistamines
Antiseptics
Artificial limbs
Aspirin
Band-Aids
Dentures
Deodorant
Disposable diapers
Eyeglasses, sunglasses, safety

glasses, soft contact lenses
Hand lotion
Hearing aids
Heart valves
Injection syringes
Insect repellent
Medical tubing
Petroleum jelly
Rubbing alcohol
Soap, shampoo
Toilet seats
Toothpaste,

toothbrushes
Vaporizers
Vitamin capsules

Other Products

Artificial colors and flavors, food preservatives
Automobile bumpers and grilles
Ballpoint pens
Boats, hulls of speedboats

Bubble gum
Cameras
Candles
Caulking
CDs, DVDs
Cleaning fluid
Clothing dyes
Combs
Computer bodies
  and hard drives
Crayons
Detergents,
  dishwashing liquid
Drinking cups
Electric blankets
Electrical tape,
  transparent tape
Fishing rods
Floor wax
Foam cushions
Footballs
  basketballs, soccer
  balls

Garden rakes
Glue
Hair curlers, hair
  dryers
Ink
Jet-plane fuel
Life jackets
Lipstick
Lunch boxes
Mops
Movie film
Nail polish
Nylon
Paint, paintbrushes,
  paint rollers
Panty hose
Parachutes
Perfume
Plastic wrap
Protective helmets
  and knee guards
Refrigerators

Rubber cement
Shoe polish
Shoes, sneakers,
  "rubber" boots,
  flip-flops
Shower curtains
Skateboards
Skis, ice skates
Soft-drink bottles
Swimming pools
Telephones
Television cabinets
Tires (synthetic
  rubber)
Toys, dollhouses
Trash bags
Umbrellas
Video games
Water pipes, water
  hoses
Waxed paper

94

Perils of Prosperity

Rising demand for oil exposed Europe, and later America, to oil shocks—serious interruptions in supply. Like a pebble tossed into a pond, an oil shock creates ripples, or effects, felt everywhere.

Oil shocks have two causes. The first is natural, because existing oil fields may not yield enough to satisfy demand. Scarcity results in higher prices for oil products, reducing our standard of living. Natural scarcity was not a problem in the world's major producing areas until recently, as we will see in the next chapter.

The second cause of oil shocks is political. Political shocks happen when governments of oil-producing countries reduce or halt supply to gain the upper hand in dealings with other governments. This is the case in the Middle East, where oil has often mixed with politics, religion, and blood. The reasons for this have shaped the history of recent times.

Foreign powers, notably Britain, controlled large areas in Africa and the Middle East for generations. British forces occupied Egypt, and a British company managed the Suez Canal, a vital waterway linking Europe and Asia. Elsewhere, British companies ran Iranian and Iraqi oil fields. Besides the oil industry, Britain also dominated the countries' governments and armed forces. However, since World War II left Britain weakened, the countries it controlled were able to gain their independence. Britain, though, still played a key role in their economies.

95

The plight of European Jews made matters more complicated. Jews had been a persecuted minority in many countries for centuries. In the 1890s, their desire for equality gave rise to Zionism. This political movement aimed at creating a Jewish state in Palestine, the Jews'

The Suez Canal at Port Said, Egypt. (1898)

Egyptian president Gamal Abdel Nasser believed that the Suez Canal belonged to Egypt as a sacred trust. (c. March 12, 1956)

ancient homeland, also called Israel or the Land of Zion. Despite objections by the Arab majority, growing numbers of Jews settled in Palestine in the 1920s, encouraged by the British government. Leaders such as Winston Churchill wanted to help Europe's Jews out of not only sympathy but necessity. These men had what critics called "oil on the brain." Should drillers find black gold in northern Iraq, they hoped to bring it to Europe by way of the Mediterranean Sea, the shortest route. It was safest, they thought, to build the future Iraqi pipeline through friendly territory—that is, across Jordan to the port of Haifa in Palestine.

Jewish immigration to Palestine became a human tidal wave due to the Holocaust, Hitler's effort to exterminate Europe's Jews during World War II. While six million Jews lost their lives, tens of thousands of survivors poured into Palestine. By the time the war ended in 1945, the British, desperate to secure their oil supplies, favored the Arab states. No matter; in 1948, the Jews defeated the armies of their Arab neighbors. Many Palestinian Arabs were expelled by force, or left on orders from their leaders. Arab states refused to recognize Israel as a country, let alone its right to exist. Their refusal has brought more wars, coupled with oil shocks.

In 1956, a British company still ran the Suez Canal and profited from its tolls on shipping. Egypt's president, military strongman Gamal Abdel Nasser, resented foreign control of the waterway. Yet, for him, the issue was broader than this. It involved a basic moral question:

Who has the better right to key assets within Egypt's boundaries—canals, bridges, railroads, ports—and the treasures that lie beneath the soil? The answer came easily to Nasser. All belonged to the Egyptian nation as sacred trusts and were not for exploitation by outsiders. Nasser decided to nationalize the Suez Canal. Nationalization means that a government takes ownership and operates foreign-held properties.

Nasser's army seized the canal and expelled its British managers. Britain saw this action as a threat to its very existence, since by 1956 two-thirds of Europe's oil passed through the canal from the Persian Gulf. "I must be absolutely blunt about the oil," said Anthony Eden, Britain's prime minister. "We could not live without oil and . . . we have no intention of being strangled to death. . . . Nasser can deny oil to Western Europe and we shall all be at his mercy."[3]

So would Israel, which in those days got its oil from Iran. Nasser had already closed the canal to Israeli shipping. Now he ordered his navy to block the Straits of Tiran, several passages formed by Red Sea islands between Egypt and Saudi Arabia. By closing the straits, Nasser prevented Israeli ships from entering the port of Eilat, a serious blow to its trade.

Britain, France, and Israel decided to overthrow Nasser. But when they attacked Egypt, he had dozens of merchant ships sunk in the canal, blocking it to all traffic. After a few weeks of fighting, the attackers agreed to a cease-fire in return for Nasser's promise to reopen the waterway and allow Israeli ships through the Straits of Tiran. Egypt kept the canal.

While the Suez crisis caused a small rise in world oil prices, it terrified companies producing Middle Eastern oil. What if Nasser decides to close the canal again, they asked, preventing us from exporting any oil? Rather than trust his goodwill, they decided to avoid the canal altogether.

Work began on a new generation of ships called supertankers. More than three times the size of a normal tanker, these were true sea monsters. Up to 1,504 feet long and 226 feet wide, they were so big that they needed at least two miles before coming to a full stop; crew members used bicycles to get around the decks. In avoiding the Suez

Canal, supertankers, laden with Persian Gulf oil, sailed around the African coast into the Atlantic Ocean, a route that added 6,500 miles to the voyage to Europe. Yet the money saved by carrying more oil offset the cost of the longer voyage. A supertanker carried two million barrels of oil, over twenty times the load of a traditional tanker.

Meanwhile, Nasser's actions had sent a thrill of pride through the Middle East. Oil-rich countries took a closer look at their concessions to foreign companies. Known as the Seven Sisters—Exxon, Mobil, Chevron, Texaco, Gulf, Royal Dutch/Shell, Anglo-Iranian Oil—those companies controlled the oil market, set prices, and gave only a small part of their profits to the host countries. That seemed unfair. So, in 1960, Iran, Iraq, Kuwait, Saudi Arabia, and Venezuela banded together to form the Organization of Petroleum Exporting Countries (OPEC).

OPEC is a cartel—that is, a group of producers that agree to work together for its members' benefit. OPEC aimed at keeping oil prices high by controlling the amount produced. To do that, its members nationalized foreign companies and took over their properties, replacing them with state-run companies. Eventually Algeria, Indonesia, Iran, Libya, Nigeria, Qatar, and the United Arab Emirates joined OPEC. The old order in Middle Eastern oil had changed and, like Humpty Dumpty, could never be put together again.

Forging the Arab Oil Weapon

Arab nations had not gotten over their 1948 defeat by Israel. It was a humiliation they felt they must avenge to regain their self-respect. Yet Israel had the support of Western nations, especially the United States, which viewed it as a key military ally in the region. To destroy Israel, then, its enemies must first destroy American support.

Nasser suggested, correctly, that without oil all the machines in the world are "mere pieces of iron, rusty, motionless, and lifeless."[4] Hitler and Japan's warlords had learned that lesson the hard way and paid for it with their lives. Now the Arabs would use their oil to discourage nations from aiding Israel or to punish any that did. Wielding the "oil weapon," Nasser insisted, would allow Arab armies to crush the Jewish state.

In 1967, the Egyptian leader formed an alliance between his country and Syria, Jordan, and Iraq. Nasser left no doubt about the alliance's goal: "We shall enter [Palestine] with its soil saturated in blood. . . . We aim at the destruction of the State of Israel."[5] After Nasser broke his promise and reclosed the Straits of Tiran to Israeli shipping, Arab armies prepared to invade. They would strike from three directions at once: from the Sinai Desert in the southwest, across the Jordan River in the east, and from Syria's Golan Heights in the north.

Words have consequences, and Israelis took Nasser's threats seriously. Rather than wait for an attack, followed by a second Holocaust, Israel struck first. June 5, 1967, became day one of what historians would later call the Six-Day War. At daybreak, Israeli air strikes caught enemy planes on the ground. By evening, the Egyptian, Syrian, Jordanian, and Iraqi air forces had become heaps of smoking junk. After Israel won control of the sky, ground forces captured the Sinai Peninsula and Gaza Strip, the West Bank of the Jordan River, East Jerusalem, and the Golan Heights. Israeli forces dug in, determined to keep these territories.

99

As the disaster unfolded, OPEC's Arab members sent their oil ministers to Baghdad for a hurried meeting. The ministers decided to punish the United States, Britain, and West Germany for supporting Israel with an embargo, or cutoff, of oil supplies. Yet the oil weapon was a blunt sword in 1967. Although the embargo lasted for months after the guns fell silent, it had no effect. America was still a major oil producer. Increased output in its fields easily offset the loss from Arab countries. The only sufferers were the Arabs, who lost income because of the embargo. Yet it soon became clear that this was the last time American oil would tip the balance in a crisis.

In 1970, Egyptian vice president Anwar el-Sadat won a bitter struggle for power following Nasser's death. Sadat and Hafez al-Assad, dictator of Syria, desperately wanted to regain the lands lost in the Six-Day War. Sadat knew of America's friendship with Israel. So he approached King Faisal Ibn Abdul Aziz, eldest son and heir of Ibn Saud. Both father and son hated Jews and wanted Israel destroyed. Ibn Saud had once declared: "For a Muslim to kill a Jew [in war], or for him to

Egyptian president Anwar el-Sadat. (c. 1980)

100

be killed by a Jew, ensures him an immediate entry in Heaven and into the august presence of God Almighty."[6] King Faisal promised to halt oil sales to the United States if it aided Israel in the event of war.

On October 6, 1973, Egyptian and Syrian armies struck without warning. It was Yom Kippur, the Day of Atonement, the holiest day in the Jewish calendar. Most Israelis were at services in synagogues, Jewish houses of worship. By the time Israeli forces massed, enemy tank columns seemed poised to retake the Golan Heights and the Sinai Peninsula. The Israelis fought hard, nearly exhausting their ammunition, particularly anti-tank shells. Israeli leaders desperately appealed to President Richard M. Nixon for a special American weapon, the TOW (tube-launched, optically tracked, wire-guided), a high-tech anti-tank missile that seldom missed its target. Nixon promised to send 4,000 TOWs in secret nighttime air operations. But the secret came out when bad weather forced the giant Hercules cargo planes to land in daylight. With the stars on their wings, nobody could mistake them for anything other than U.S. aircraft.

Now OPEC's Arab members, led by Saudi Arabia, made good on King Faisal's threat. As fighting raged, they halted oil shipments to the United States, the Netherlands, Portugal, and South Africa, all friends of Israel. This time the Arab boycott bit—hard and deep. By the 1970s, America was no longer producing as much oil as in the past. World War II and the postwar economic boom had sharply reduced its oil reserves. Although it still had plenty of oil, it needed ever more

Middle Eastern oil to fill the gap between its production and needs. For example, 85 percent of Americans drove to work each day.

America experienced its first oil shock. Within days of the cutoff, oil prices rose from $2.90 to $11.65 a barrel; gasoline prices soared from 20 cents to $1.20 a gallon, an all-time high. Across America, fuel shortages forced factories to close early and airlines to cancel flights. Filling stations posted signs: "Sorry, No Gas Today." If a station did have gasoline, motorists lined up before sunrise to buy a few gallons; owners limited the amount sold to each customer. Motorists grew impatient. Fistfights broke out and, occasionally, gunfire. President Nixon called for America to end its dependence on foreign oil. "Let us set as our national goal . . . that by the end of this decade we will have developed the potential to meet our own energy needs without depending on any foreign energy source," he said.[7] We have still not met this goal.

Meantime, a secret British government report warned that if things grew worse, American forces would seize Saudi Arabian and

101

A new gas-rationing system is announced. (c. January 1974)

Kuwaiti oil fields.[8] Yet that did not happen for two reasons. First, the Israelis used massive air strikes and American TOW missiles to destroy enemy tank formations. Having turned the tide of battle, they decided to obey a cease-fire order by the United Nations. Second, while the embargo continued for five months after the cease-fire took effect, the oil companies learned how to evade it. The embargo had a flaw: it applied only to Israel's friends. This allowed the companies that carried oil in their supertankers to take it from OPEC's non-Arab members to wherever they pleased. For example, Iran, though a Muslim country and OPEC member, was not an Arab country. It refused to take part in the embargo and even increased production to cash in on higher oil prices. No one dreamed then that the next oil shock would come from Iran.

Iran: From Shah to Ayatollah

After World War I, Britain extended control over Iran from its military bases in neighboring Iraq. British troops occupied all major cities. British officials replaced the unreliable shah with Reza Pahlavi, an army officer they trusted to run things their way. Though a murderous thug who ruled by terror (he threw bakers into their ovens for charging higher prices than the government ordered), Shah Reza was a shrewd man. Shortly before World War II began, he persuaded Britain to withdraw its forces. But since Shah Reza admired Hitler, in 1941 British and Russian forces invaded Iran and overthrew him. The British replaced Shah Reza with his son, Mohammad Reza Pahlavi. Following Hitler's defeat, the Allies withdrew their forces.

Iran remained a troubled country. While Shah Mohammad Reza Pahlavi, his supporters, and a few wealthy families lived lavishly, ordinary Iranians suffered terribly. Farmers worked long and hard, virtual slaves to landowners. Unemployment and poverty soared in the cities, even in Tehran, the capital. Millions of families could not afford to send their children to school. To improve living conditions would have cost lots of money that the country did not have.

Iranians resented their lack of control of their national treasure, oil. By the 1950s, Abadan held the world's largest refinery. It covered most of the desert island, barren except for fractionating towers, tank farms, pipelines, warehouses, and workers' living quarters. The Anglo-Iranian Oil Company ran Abadan for the benefit of its private investors and its chief shareholder, the British government, to which it also paid taxes. Its British employees lived like royalty, in segregated communities with signs that read "Not for Iranians." A visitor described how native workers lived:

> Wages were fifty cents a day. There was no vacation pay, no sick leave, no disability compensation. The workers lived in a shanty-town called . . . Paper City, without running water or electricity. . . . In winter the earth flooded and became a flat, perspiring lake. . . . Summer was worse. . . . The heat was torrid, the worst I've ever known—sticky and unrelenting—while the wind and sandstorms whipped off the desert hot as a [blowtorch]. . . . In the British section of Abadan there were lawns, rose beds, tennis courts, swimming pools and clubs; in [Paper City] there was nothing—not a tea shop, not a bath, not a single tree.[9]

103

Patriots led by Mohammad Mossadegh gave voice to popular grievances. A lawyer by profession, Mossadegh was a leader in parliament. "The oil resources of Iran, like its soil, its rivers and mountains, are the property of the people of Iran," he insisted. "They alone have the authority to decide what shall be done with it, by whom and how."[10] That was only simple justice, he thought.

Iranian prime minister Mohammad Mossadegh. (c. 1965)

In 1951, Mossadegh, now prime minister, had parliament pass a law nationalizing the oil industry. Outraged, the British declared economic warfare on Iran. Britain removed its skilled technicians, forcing the Abadan refinery to close. Royal Navy warships halted tankers on the high seas because they carried "stolen" Iranian oil. When Mossadegh refused to give in, the British decided to overthrow him. In August 1953, however, he uncovered the plot, broke all relations with Britain, and closed its Tehran embassy. The plot collapsed.

Since they could not overthrow Mossadegh by themselves, the British turned to America. The prime minister must go, officials said, not only to protect Britain's oil interests but also to prevent a possible Russian takeover of Iran and the Persian Gulf states. The 1950s saw the height of the Cold War, a time of intense rivalry between Communist nations led by Russia and the democracies led by the United States. The rivalry was "cold" because it did not lead to fighting, or "hot" war, between the two groups. President Dwight D. Eisenhower agreed that the "free world" must save Iran and its oil or face disaster. For, he said, as surely as day follows night, a Russian takeover would bring World War III and the probable extermination of the human race by atomic weapons.

Kermit Roosevelt Jr., super-spook, was Theodore Roosevelt's grandson and Franklin Roosevelt's nephew, and the head of the CIA's Middle Eastern division. (c. 1950)

Eisenhower ordered the Central Intelligence Agency (CIA) into action. A top-secret organization, the CIA gathers information, called intelligence, on foreign governments and groups such as terrorists. The CIA also conducts secret operations overseas. These have included overthrowing unfriendly governments, spying, kidnapping, and assassinations. Iran was the organization's first successful overthrow operation.

Kermit Roosevelt Jr. headed the CIA's Middle Eastern division. The grandson of former president Theodore Roosevelt and nephew of former president Franklin Roosevelt, Kim, as friends called him, was a mild-mannered man with thick eyeglasses and a ready smile. He seemed so ordinary that a friend said he was "the last person you would expect to be up to his neck in dirty tricks."[11] In other words, Kim was the ideal "spook," or secret agent.

The master trickster and his team set up headquarters in the basement of the U.S. embassy in Tehran. They freely spent American tax dollars to hatch a plot against a legally elected head of state. The idea was to use various Iranian groups to create a crisis. Kermit's agents bribed newspaper editors to print articles describing the prime minister as a drug-addicted lunatic; an emotional man, Mossadegh wept in public when deeply moved. Agents hired heads of criminal gangs, thugs like Shaban the Brainless, to chant pro-Mossadegh slogans and start riots in his name. Meanwhile, they hired other gangs to fight them in the name of the shah. Finally, Kermit bribed army officers to "restore order" by force. On August 19, 1953, Shah Mohammad Reza Pahlavi fired the prime minister. After serving a three-year prison term for trying to overthrow the shah—a lie—Mossadegh spent his final years under house arrest, dying in 1967 at the age of eighty-five. Kermit later became an important figure in the American oil industry, first as a vice president of the Gulf Oil Company, then by selling his "expertise" on Middle Eastern affairs to oil companies and other businesses.

With the fall of Mossadegh, Anglo-Iranian Oil Company officials expected to return to their old ways. It was not to be. The company, renamed British Petroleum (BP), had to join European and American firms in sharing half their oil profits among themselves, the other half with the Iranian government. Yet toppling Mossadegh would cost America dearly. When the truth about the plot came out, Iranians hated America and the shah as its "puppet."

Mohammad Reza Pahlavi took over as shah of Iran after his father was forced to abdicate the throne. (c. 1973)

106

A British diplomat once said that the flood of oil money made Iran's ruler "silly." This was because Shah Mohammad Reza Pahlavi used only a tiny portion of it to help his people. Much of the oil money went to satisfy His Majesty's ego and lust for power. Fortunes were poured into magnificent palaces for and monuments to Iran's "Light of the Sun," as he insisted upon being called. To turn Iran into a world power, he spent billions on weapons, mostly bought from America. CIA agents trained his secret police, experts at making opponents "disappear."

The U.S. government wanted a strong Iran to keep the oil flowing, at good prices, to America and its European allies. It found all sorts of creative excuses to justify the shah's oppressive rule. On December 31, 1977, at a banquet in the shah's honor, President Jimmy Carter toasted the Iranian ruler. "Iran under the great leadership of the shah," said Carter, "is an island of stability in one of the most troubled areas of the world. This is a great tribute to you, Your

Ayatollah Ruhollah Khomeini led a terrorist regime against "impure" Muslims. (c. 1979)

Majesty, and to your leadership. And to the respect, admiration and love which your people give to you."[12] Carter could not have been more wrong. The shah's Iran was *not* an island of stability. The typical person in the Iranian street despised the Light of the Sun. Opposition to him grew more outspoken, more violent.

The shah's opponents united behind Ayatollah Ruhollah Khomeini. (An ayatollah is a high-ranking Muslim religious scholar and leader.) Khomeini detested the shah as a false Muslim, a demon tied to the "Great Satan," his name for America. In April 1979, Khomeini led a mass uprising that forced the shah to flee Iran. Stricken with cancer, the dying man went to the United States for treatment. Iranians had never forgiven America for turning its embassy into a "den of spies." So, when the shah arrived in the United States, a mob of armed "students" broke into the embassy in Tehran and seized sixty employees as hostages. The hostages, they said, would be returned only after President Jimmy Carter returned the shah to his homeland for trial. Iran's last shah died the next year in exile in Egypt, but the hostages spent 444 days in captivity before being released the day the next president, Ronald Reagan, took office.

Ayatollah Khomeini declared Iran an Islamic republic. In reality, it was a religious dictatorship under the "Government of God," or Islamic law as understood by religious leaders. Anyone who challenged Khomeini's—that is, God's—authority faced punishment as severe as any inflicted by the shah. On Khomeini's orders, the Government of God abolished freedom of the press, outlawed political parties, and limited personal freedoms, even dictating how citizens might "properly" dress and wear their hair. Resisters faced firing squads.

Unlike the shah, who wanted to make Iran a world power, the ayatollah wanted Iran to conquer the world for God. As he put it: "We will export our revolution throughout the world . . . until the calls 'there is no God but God and Muhammad is the messenger of God' are echoed all over the world."[13] God, Khomeini said, expected nothing less of His followers. They must be willing to kill, and to be killed, in His name.

Khomeini began with terrorism against "impure" Muslims, Iran's

Arab neighbors. Iranian agents planted bombs in Kuwait and Saudi Arabia, while assassination squads killed local officials. The ayatollah's chief target, however, was Iraq.

Enter Saddam Hussein

Many Iraqis wanted independence from Britain. Under pressure from Iraqi patriots, the British government signed a treaty with King Faisal in 1930. The treaty promised British military protection against foreign attack and eventual independence for Iraq. In return, Iraq allowed Britain to station troops and have air bases on its soil. Two years later, Britain recognized Iraqi independence. When World War II began in 1939, British forces seized power to prevent a takeover by Iraqi army officers friendly to Hitler. At the end of the war, British forces finally left Iraq.

108

Things did not go well for the oil-rich nation. Like Iran, Iraq suffered from a wide income gap between its wealthy minority and poor majority. In 1958, army officers overthrew the last king, Faisal II, butchered him and his family, and declared Iraq a republic. After years of political infighting, Saddam Hussein became president in July 1979. Like Ayatollah Khomeini, who overthrew the shah three months earlier, he became a dictator.

Saddam Hussein had two sides to his nature. The good Saddam built roads, opened free schools for all Iraqi children, saw that illiterate adults learned to read, and gave everyone free medical care. The bad Saddam was a monster whose secret police tortured and killed countless "enemies," burying them in unmarked

Saddam Hussein appearing on Iraqi television. (date unknown)

mass graves in the desert.

Khomeini sent agents to murder Iraqi officials and stir up trouble in the Kurdish region of northern Iraq. Unless he struck first, Saddam feared being overthrown, followed by a bullet in the head. He had no desire to conquer Iran, but wanted a short war to end the Iranian threat. In September 1980, Iraqi forces suddenly invaded Iran. Nobody expected the bloodshed to last eight years.

Though Saddam's forces advanced easily at first, Iran recovered quickly. Khomeini ordered "human-wave" attacks, mass assaults on Iraqi positions without artillery or air support. Iranian soldiers went to the front carrying their own coffins, for the ayatollah told them that "the purest joy in Islam is to kill and be killed for God." Khomeini also urged thousands of boys as young as twelve to become "martyrs" in the "holy war" and gave them "Passports to Paradise," plastic keys their spirits could use to unlock the gates of heaven. Iraqi soldiers could hardly believe their eyes. An officer reported:

> They chant "Allahu Akbar" [God Is Great] and they keep coming, and we keep shooting. . . . My men are eighteen, nineteen, just a few years older than these kids. I've seen them crying, and at times the officers have to kick them back to their guns.[14]

As the war dragged on, it seemed that Iran might win and, worse, occupy Saudi Arabia and Kuwait. Terrified, these oil-rich countries gave or lent Saddam billions of dollars for his war effort. President Ronald Reagan, Carter's successor, saw the Iranian danger, too. "There is no way that we can stand by and see [Saudi Arabia] taken over by anyone who would shut off the oil," he said. "An attack on Saudi Arabia would be considered an attack on the United States."[15] To check Iran, Reagan secretly aided Iraq. The Defense Intelligence Agency sent officers to Baghdad with detailed plans for an offensive against Iran. Meanwhile, the CIA jammed Iranian radar to protect Iraqi warplanes and gave Iraq satellite photos of Iranian army positions.

Reagan even turned a blind eye to a human tragedy. Since many

109

Kurdish people hoped an Iranian victory would allow them to break away from Iraq and form their own nation, Saddam began the al-Anfal (Spoils of War) campaign. Iraqi ground troops killed as many as 200,000 Kurdish civilians and destroyed over 3,800 Kurdish villages. Iraqi planes dropped poison gas on thirty Kurdish villages and towns. In the largest town, Halabjah, gas killed 3,200 to 5,000 people, including children and babies; many dead babies were later found in the arms of their dead mothers. American journalist Patrick Tyler visited Halabjah soon after the attack. He reported:

> The town was silent, seemingly empty at first. Then we saw hundreds of bodies in all manner of everyday poses. . . . One powerful image was a grandfather clutching an infant on a doorstep. Another family lay on the ground in a courtyard with the lunch table still set and food rotting. . . . [We saw] the bodies of a dozen or so small girls. . . . They lay like dolls splayed randomly on the gravel bed, eyes open in some cases, staring skyward. The faces seemed to beckon, as if impatient for the living to gather them in.[16]

110

In Baghdad, American diplomats protested against the outrage privately but did nothing to stop it.

Oil, as ever, was the chief consideration. Iraqi aircraft bombed the Abadan refinery; Iranian aircraft bombed the refinery at Basra. Worse, the "tanker war" threatened to halt oil shipments from the Persian Gulf. Iraq began by attacking Iranian tankers. Iran went further. It threatened tankers of any Gulf nation that supported Iraq. This was no bluff. The Iranian navy placed mines in the shipping lanes used by Kuwait. Iranian speedboats raked Kuwaiti tankers with machine-gun fire.

Oil prices rose steeply, as a new shock threatened the world economy. To secure Persian Gulf oil, President Reagan ordered an aircraft-carrier battle group into the Indian Ocean, within striking distance of Iran. American destroyers cleared Iranian mines. Other warships escorted Kuwaiti tankers through the dangerous waters.

A family surveying the remains of a destroyed Kurdish village in Iraq, which is still a turbulent area more than twenty years after Hussein's al-Anfal campaign. (c. 2009)

111

Each tanker flew the Stars and Stripes. Thus, an attack on it would be an attack on America. When Iran tested American resolve by firing on a Kuwaiti tanker, the U.S. Navy destroyed Iranian patrol boats.

Finally, in August 1988, after eight years and 950,000 military deaths on both sides, the United Nations arranged a cease-fire. But the cease-fire was merely a breathing space between wars.

America's Oil Wars

Saddam Hussein realized that the Iran-Iraq war had cost so much Iraqi blood and treasure that he faced open rebellion. To save himself, he had to rebuild Iraq. And to rebuild, he needed lots of money. In Saddam's eyes, he was a hero, because he had protected Kuwait and Saudi Arabia from the fanatical Iranians. Now he demanded payment. Both countries must cancel his war debts and help pay the cost of rebuilding Iraq. Kuwait must go further. He accused the tiny country of stealing Iraqi oil from a field just across the border. Nevertheless, Kuwait demanded its money and, rightly, dismissed the charge of stealing. On August 2, 1990, Iraqi forces invaded Kuwait. Within days they overran its defenders and moved tanks close to the Saudi Arabian border. Overnight, Saddam's action turned a onetime friend of the United States into an enemy.

President George H. W. Bush, Ronald Reagan's successor, saw Saddam's aggression as a threat to every oil-importing nation. Combined with Iraq's oil, that of Kuwait and Saudi Arabia would give the dictator control of more than half the world's reserves. "Our jobs, our way of life, our own freedom and the freedom of friendly countries around the world would all suffer if control of the world's great oil reserves fell into the hands of Saddam Hussein," said Bush.[17] To keep that from happening, he rallied fifty-seven nations, including OPEC members, against Iraq.

Saddam promised that if war came he would unleash the "mother of all battles," ending in a smashing Iraqi victory. He did nothing of the sort. In February 1991, after a furious air assault, American-led forces liberated Kuwait in 100 hours.

What Saddam did unleash was ecoterrorism, the destruction of the environment upon which life depends by terrorist nations or groups. Retreating Iraqi forces set fire to all 640 Kuwaiti oil wells and dumped 9.5 million barrels (399 million gallons) of crude oil into the Persian Gulf, causing history's worst oil spill. The accumulation of oil lakes and black, greasy soot from the burning wells made hundreds of square miles of Kuwait uninhabitable. Spilled oil all but ruined the Persian Gulf fishing industry, a key food source in the region. Floating sheets of oil spoiled 440 miles of the Saudi Arabian coastline, killing countless shrimp, fish, and turtles. It took American and British experts a year to put out the well fires. Parts of the Persian Gulf still have not recovered from the oil spills.

Despite losing a war and causing an environmental disaster, Saddam would stay in power another twelve years. His end came because of an event he neither ordered nor even knew about beforehand.

9/11 and After

On September 11, 2001, terrorists flew two hijacked airliners into the towers of the World Trade Center in New York City. Other terrorists crashed an airliner into the Pentagon in Washington, D.C., and another hijacked plane was diverted into an empty field in Pennsylvania as passengers fought back. It turned out that fourteen of the nineteen suicide-murderers were Saudi Arabians. Shocked Americans asked why citizens of a country their forces had defended should kill over 3,000 innocent people. Why, indeed?

Oil has two nicknames, "black gold" and "the devil's tears," because it brings wealth and trouble. Saudi Arabia is a glaring example of the social problems that can come from oil wealth. Ibn Saud, we recall,

113

Firefighters raising the American flag at Ground Zero.
(September 11, 2001)

conquered Arabia with the help of Wahhabi warriors. These devout Muslims rejected modern ideas and ways as unholy, corrupting, and sinful. So when oil wealth allowed Ibn Saud to introduce modern products—automobiles, telephones, radios—they rebelled. Although he crushed the rebellion, Wahhabi resentment still ran strong and deep.

Ibn Saud's sons, grandsons, and other male relatives spent vast amounts of oil money on luxuries. Sprawling palaces with hundreds of air-conditioned rooms, banquet halls, gardens, and fountains rose in the cities. Saudi princes bought fleets of fancy cars and lavish yachts. They vacationed in Europe, where they gambled and drank whiskey, forbidden by the Koran, Islam's holy book. Soon after Ayatollah Khomeini overthrew the shah in Iran, Wahhabi rebels seized the Grand Mosque in Mecca, Islam's holiest site. After heavy fighting, royal forces recaptured the mosque. However, since the Wahhabi threat remained, Saudi leaders decided to buy peace with oil money. They agreed to fund Wahhabi schools across the globe that would teach about Islam—but also would preach hatred of unbelievers and "bad" Muslims. They also struck an unofficial deal: the Wahhabi could make trouble wherever they wished, only not in Saudi Arabia. In short, Saudi oil profits fueled terrorism.

The chief Saudi terrorist was Osama bin Laden, son of a wealthy building contractor. Bin Laden formed al-Qaeda, Arabic for "the Base," a terrorist organization with branches throughout

Osama bin Laden, founder of the terrorist organization al-Qaeda. (c. 1997)

the Middle East and in most European countries. Al-Qaeda and its Afghan allies, the Taliban (or "Students"), controlled Afghanistan, a chaotic country bordering Russia to the north and Pakistan to the south. Afghanistan became a terrorist stronghold. Bin Laden used gifts from Saudi Arabia and other Muslim countries to build terrorist training camps and plan attacks on unbelievers across the globe.

When it became clear that bin Laden was behind the attacks of September 11, 2001, President George W. Bush declared the war on terror. He began by ordering American forces to invade Afghanistan. While they quickly occupied the country, bin Laden and many al-Qaeda and Taliban fighters fled into the mountains along the Afghanistan-Pakistan border. To this day, they continue to fight American and NATO soldiers in the rugged border region. Bin Laden was tracked down and killed by American commandos while hiding in Pakistan in May 2011.

115

Next the president turned to Iraq. While there was no evidence of an Iraqi alliance with bin Laden, American officials accused Saddam Hussein of developing atomic, chemical, and biological weapons, a charge later disproved by captured documents and on-site inspections. War, officials argued, was necessary because the dictator might use those weapons against the Persian Gulf states, even Europe and America. The war on Iraq, said Secretary of Defense Donald Rumsfeld, "has nothing to do with oil," since "the oil wells belong to the Iraqi people."[18] It was for self-defense, to overthrow a tyrant, and to bring democracy to the Middle East.

But is the war on terror really the war for oil in disguise? Critics think so. In February 2003, a poster issued by the anti-war group DemocracyMeansYou.com portrayed leading American and British oil companies behind the drive for war. The poster had President Bush say: "We SHELL not EXXONerate Saddam Hussein for his actions. We will MOBILize to meet this threat in the Persian GULF until an AMOCOble solution is reached. Our plan is to BPrepared. Failing that, we ARCOming to kick his ass."

Critics also quote high U.S. government officials to prove their point. Take Alan Greenspan, former chairman of the Federal Reserve, the government agency that oversees the nation's banking system. In 2007, Greenspan declared Saddam Hussein's removal "essential" to secure the world's oil supplies. "The Iraq War," he added, "is largely about oil."[19]

Despite decades of British control, Iraq has never been fully explored for oil. Only 2,300 wells have been drilled there, compared to around one million wells in Texas alone. Iraq has top-grade crude oil, high in carbon and low in sulfur. This may explain why, after American troops took Baghdad, officers immediately placed guards around the Oil Ministry; it held thousands of geological maps, vital for future oil exploration. Meanwhile, American troops stood by as mobs looted the National Library and the National Museum of Archaeology, treasure-houses filled with ancient books and relics. No wonder war critics insist that Saddam Hussein's overthrow was the first step in "turning a 'friendly' Iraq into a private American oil pumping station."[20] We will not learn the full truth until the government makes secret documents available to the American public, if it ever does.

116

Oil may also have played a key role in the decision to invade Afghanistan. Most people in the region say the war on terror "is all about oil." Huge untapped oil reserves lie in Central Asia, under the Caspian Sea, the world's largest landlocked body of water, and the lands to its east.

Central Asian nations—Kazakhstan, Kyrgyzstan, Tajikistan, Turkmenistan—lack the money and know-how to develop these reserves on their own. Besides, getting the oil from the ground would be the easiest step, for a pipeline would then have to carry it away. Russia's money, know-how, and a pipeline across its territory to European markets would give it control of a precious natural resource and thus unmatched political power. However, American money, know-how, and a pipeline across Afghanistan to Pakistani ports on the Arabian Sea would open Indian and Chinese markets to American oil companies trading in Central Asian oil.[21]

It seems that oil, wealth, and war will be bound together forever. Yet things are not always what they seem, and forever is a long time. It is more likely that the black stuff that fuels our world will become scarcer, forcing us to learn to live with less, or none at all.

VII

A DAY OF RECKONING

The world's oil addiction is hastening a day of reckoning. Humanity's way of life is on a collision course with geology—with the stark fact that the earth holds a finite supply of oil. The flood of crude from fields around the world will ultimately top out, then dwindle.

—Tim Appenzeller
Science Editor, National Geographic

Beyond Middle Eastern Oil

The shocks of the 1960s and 1970s forced explorers to step up the search for oil outside the Middle East. To search more effectively, they learned to "see" underground with seismographs, devices that record movements beneath the earth's surface. Geologists had used the seismograph for decades to study earthquakes and volcanoes. Oil explorers adopted the device to locate likely reservoirs. After drilling a hole, they insert an explosive charge. Shock waves from the explosion travel through the ground, bouncing off the rock layers. The pattern of shock waves, recorded by computers, can locate an oil reservoir. Vibrator, or "thumper," trucks work the same way, but without explosives. Each truck has a metal pad underneath. When the truck stops, the pad raises it, supporting its full weight. The truck then vibrates, setting off shock waves.

In 1967, these methods helped find oil at Prudhoe Bay on the northern coast of Alaska, bordering the Arctic Ocean. Prudhoe Bay is the largest oil field ever discovered in North America, larger by half than Texas's Black Giant field. To bring the oil to market, workers built an 800-mile pipeline across Alaska, to the port of Valdez on the Pacific Ocean. From there, supertankers take it to refineries in California.

Explorers also discovered oil in deep offshore waters. Finding oil under the ocean floor is a lot like finding it on land. However, instead of explosives and thumper trucks, explorers have ships equipped with high-pressure air guns that send bursts of bubbles slamming into the ocean floor. The bubbles create shock waves that microphones towed behind the ships detect and send to onboard computers, which turn the rock layers into digital images. In the 1970s, explorers discovered major oil fields in the North Sea, the Gulf of Mexico, and the North Atlantic, as well as off the west coast of Africa.

118

Drilling for oil in deep water is not easy or safe. Explorers begin by building a platform—that is, a structure designed for drilling and extracting oil. Depending on local conditions, the platform either is attached to the seabed in various ways or floats above the drilling site, held in place by huge anchors. All platforms, however, have living quarters for workers, mess halls, lifeboats, drilling machinery, and a helipad, a place for helicopters to land and take off from.

Some platforms face unique challenges. Ocean Ranger, for example, stood in the North Atlantic off Canada's east coast. Seamen call this area Iceberg Alley because floating mountains of ice often drift into the shipping lanes. To deal with them, engineers built a platform weighing nearly 600,000 tons, heavier than five aircraft carriers, resting on massive steel and concrete supporting columns. A visitor wrote:

Towering thirty-seven stories from keel to derrick top,
moored by twelve anchors with cables each a mile long, the
Ranger seemed a temple of stability. Veteran ship captains
were amazed to find that she hardly rocked at all. . . . But

the oil men who ran the Ocean Ranger just propped up their cowboy boots and smiled. Well, Oklahoma didn't move around under your feet, either.[1]

Engineers thought Ocean Ranger "unsinkable." It was not, because nobody can imagine, let alone prepare for, every problem. Nature has a way of defeating our best efforts. Accident, error, stupidity, and bad luck always play a role in human affairs. That is what happened in February 1982, when a huge wave found Ocean Ranger's weak spot. Water poured through an open porthole, causing a power failure that put the pumps out of action. Ocean Ranger toppled over and sank,

119

An oil platform in the Gulf of Mexico. (2004)

120

The *Exxon Valdez* supertanker two days after tearing its hull on a reef. (March 27, 1989)

taking eighty-four workers with it. Six years later, Piper Alpha, a platform in the North Sea off the coast of Scotland, exploded after a worker forgot to close a natural-gas valve. Out of a crew of 226, only 59 survived, making Piper Alpha the deadliest platform disaster ever.

Supertankers are more fragile than oil platforms. Nicknamed "floating balloons" because their hulls are so thin, they are so expensive to run that a day's delay can cost owners many thousands of dollars. Thus, owners urge captains to "make time"—that is, go fast even in dangerous waters. That spelled trouble for the *Valdez*, flagship of the Exxon tanker fleet. On March 24, 1989, the *Valdez* sailed from its home port, Valdez, Alaska, heading south. During the night, Captain Joseph Hazelwood veered out of the regular sea-lane to avoid a reported iceberg. Next day, the *Valdez* struck a reef, tearing its hull and spilling 261,905 barrels of oil into Prince William Sound. Hazelwood was charged with being drunk on duty, but a jury found him not guilty owing to lack of evidence. Whether he was drunk or not, the damage was done. Scientists believe it will take decades for the shoreline and wildlife of Prince William Sound to recover from the spill, if ever. Yet some good came from the *Valdez* disaster. Congress passed a law saying only supertankers with double bottoms, for double strength, can enter American waters.

Despite platform and tanker accidents, the 1980s and 1990s were a happy time for oil users. Some OPEC nations cheated; greedy for profits, they produced more oil than they had pledged to OPEC's other members. Production from Alaskan and offshore fields swelled world supplies, lowering prices, too. At times, oil cost less than bottled water.

"In the U.S., we get fired up about doing something when oil prices are high, then when prices drop, we forget about it," said business leader Fred Tennant. He was right. Low prices ended efforts to save oil or find substitutes for it. Instead, car sales soared. During the 1990s, Americans bought a new car every three seconds; a new baby came into the world every eight seconds. Studies showed that adults spent more time in their

121

An oil-covered sea otter in the aftermath of the *Exxon Valdez* spill. (March 25, 1989)

cars than with their children. Bigger was better, as gas-guzzling SUVs clogged highways and hogged parking spaces. Still, the good times could not last forever. They never do.[2]

Hubbert's Peak

A hidden crisis is part of the very nature of oil. An oil field is like a person. It, too, has a life cycle, passing from birth and maturity through old age to death. This is no problem, if explorers find new fields to replace the dead ones. Yet fossil fuels are not renewable. Once we burn them, they are gone. Surely, oil and coal are forming as you read these words. However, since they need millions of years to mature, we cannot use them for millions of years. Humanity cannot afford to wait that long.

In young fields, we recall, drilling releases pressure in the reservoir rocks, allowing oil to rise to the surface on its own. But as a field ages, the loss of oil reduces pressure. When this happens, workers take drilling rigs apart, put them on trucks, and haul them to another site or storage facility. In their place, they install electrically powered pumps to lift oil to the surface. Nicknamed "nodding donkeys," these pumps look like donkeys from a distance. Each pump's driving beam slowly swings up and down, sending a plunger into the well. As the "donkey head" rises, the plunger draws oil to the surface.

Gradually, however, pumping becomes less effective. To maintain pressure, workers inject water to wash the black droplets out of the

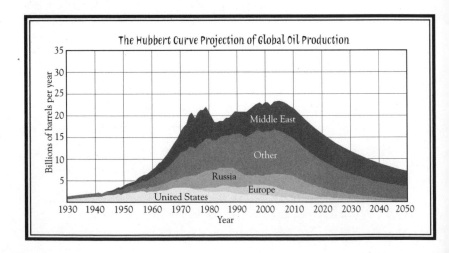

The Hubbert Curve Projection of Global Oil Production

pores in reservoir rocks. This method eventually fails, too, and oil flow stops. Despite the fact that the field is considered dead, at least half its oil is still in the reservoir, because we do not know how to get it out. Though the American oil industry, for example, has produced about 160 billion barrels of oil since 1859, some 330 billion barrels remain underground, beyond reach.

Scientist M. King Hubbert took a proven fact—that oil fields have a life cycle—a step further. Oil-industry people call his discovery Hubbert's peak. You cannot find it on a map, for it is not a place but the top, or peak, of a curve on a graph. Hubbert's studies showed that despite increased production, the amount of oil available will eventually reach its peak and then taper off.

In 1956, Hubbert warned that U.S. oil production would peak in the early 1970s, followed by oil production in the rest of the world between the years 2006 and 2017. Hubbert's prediction seems to be coming true. American production topped out in 1971; since then, we have had to import ever-larger amounts, chiefly from the Middle East. A recent U.S. government report bluntly said, "World oil reserves are being depleted three times as fast as they are being discovered. Oil is being produced from past discoveries, but the reserves are not being fully replaced. Remaining oil reserves of individual oil companies must continue to shrink."[3] But while the supply of oil is growing smaller, world population is expected to rise from 6.8 billion in the year 2010 to 9.3 billion by 2050. More people want more oil than ever before. Burgeoning economies in China and India demand it to fuel more cars, factories, and electrical power plants.

Failure to meet the peak-oil challenge while there is still time will make things worse. Some experts predict a day of reckoning— doomsday—when modern societies will collapse like houses of cards for lack of oil. A new dark age will follow, they claim, a nightmare era of scarcity, poverty, and violence lasting centuries:

> Permanent fuel shortages would tip the world into
> generations-long economic depression. Millions would
> lose their jobs as industry implodes. . . . Energy wars would

123

flare. . . . The underpinnings of our civilization will start tumbling like dominos. The price of houses will collapse. Stock markets will crash. Within a short period, human wealth . . . will shrivel. . . . Once affluent cities with street cafés will have [lines] at soup kitchens and armies of beggars. The crime rate will soar. . . . [Fanatics] will rise, feeding on the anger of the newly poor and whipping up support. The new rulers will find the tools of repression—emergency laws, prison camps, a relaxed attitude toward torture—already in place, courtesy of the war on terror.[4]

124

World population would crash without the black stuff. Oil refineries, we recall, make ammonia, the key ingredient in chemical fertilizers for farming. It follows that less oil means less fertilizer, bringing the green revolution in food production to a screeching halt. Its end, in turn, would bring starvation to millions across the globe. It would also mean the end of plastics and other oil-based products we depend upon. Advanced medical treatments rely on high-tech machines that are worthless without the energy to run them.

A Dangerous World

Oil influences the balance of power in the world, too. The United States has an "energy-intensive" economy and society. The numbers speak for themselves:

- Our country has 5 percent of the world's population but uses 26 percent of its energy.
- As of 2008, Americans used seventeen million barrels of oil each day.
- It takes seven gallons of gasoline per person— man, woman, and child—to run the country each day.
- We burn one out of every seven barrels of oil produced in the world on our highways.
- Drivers waste twelve million barrels of oil each year stalled in traffic jams.[5]

More than ever, oil is the "blood of battles." The amount of fuel used by the war machines of World War II is small in comparison with today's demands. In the 2003 Iraq war, for example, the forces that defeated Saddam Hussein burned over three million gallons of oil and gasoline each day. A sixty-eight-ton Abrams tank, backbone of our armored forces, burns one gallon of fuel every half mile. A B-52 bomber needs 3,000 gallons of fuel an hour. Tanker planes are "flying filling stations" that pump 600 gallons of kerosene-based jet fuel a minute into each thirsty warplane. It costs $840 per day to deliver the fuel to support one soldier in oil-rich Iraq.[6]

We are walking on a greased tightrope. Most of the world's known offshore fields have already peaked, along with the giant Alaskan oil field. The aging fields of Saudi Arabia and Kuwait are in decline, too. There is a popular Saudi Arabian saying: "My father rode a camel, I and my sons drive cars, my grandsons will ride camels."

125

This does not mean the Persian Gulf countries are running out of oil just yet, only that it has become harder and more expensive to produce. They will still have 83 percent of the world's proven oil reserves by the year 2020. This is not a good thing for America; experts call it "the energy equivalent of nuclear weapons." For oil empowers those who do not wish us well.[7]

The U.S. Marines performing a pre-mission check on an Abrams tank in Camp Fallujah, Iraq. (January 21, 2007)

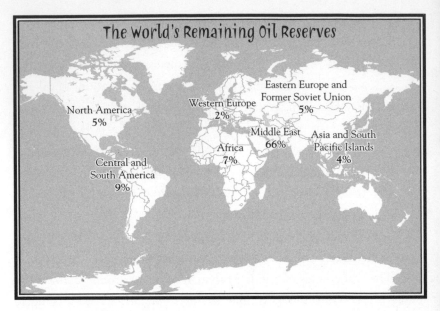

The World's Remaining Oil Reserves

North America
5%

Western Europe
2%

Eastern Europe and
Former Soviet Union
5%

Middle East
66%

Asia and South
Pacific Islands
4%

Africa
7%

Central and
South America
9%

126

Our oil addiction has caused the greatest, swiftest transfer of wealth in history. Each year we spend $700 billion on foreign oil, and the amount keeps growing. This is a tax on every American—one that we did not vote for and cannot afford. Countries like Saudi Arabia have fed billions of our oil dollars to terrorist groups, who use them to mount attacks on us. Equally important, buying foreign oil reduces our buying power at home. And reduced consumer buying power translates into lost manufacturing jobs. Every $1 billion spent on foreign oil costs America 27,000 jobs each year, economists believe. Any political upheaval in an oil-producing region can send crude oil prices soaring. In March 2011, for example, a revolution aimed at deposing Libyan dictator Colonel Muammar Gaddafi caused the price of a barrel of crude to "spike" by a dollar or two within a few days. (Rebels captured the dictator and shot him to death in October 2011.) Thus, reliance on foreign oil threatens our prosperity and security—no, our entire way of life. This is serious; some authorities say it is worse than losing a major war.

VIII

FOSSIL FUELS AND THE NATURAL ENVIRONMENT

The earth lies polluted under its inhabitants;
for they have transgressed laws,
violated the statutes,
broken the everlasting covenant.

—Isaiah 24:5

Harmful Environmental Effects

While we enjoy the many benefits of oil, these do not come without heavy costs to Earth's natural environment. Indeed, some experts have argued that the damage done not only by oil but by all fossil fuels far outweighs the benefits.

BP's Deepwater Horizon disaster, the *Exxon Valdez* accident, and Saddam Hussein's criminal dumping of oil into the Persian Gulf are frightful reminders of how spills can harm wildlife. True, every year natural seeps release more oil in the world's waters than man-made spills ever have. Yet there is a difference. Natural spills are not very destructive, because individual seeps ooze out slowly and are small, allowing bacteria and evaporation to break down the oil before it can do any serious damage. However, man-made spills happen suddenly and in large, concentrated amounts that may linger for years if they reach shore.

The Deepwater Horizon Disaster

During the evening of Tuesday, April 20, 2010, Micah Sandell sat in the cab of his crane thirty feet above the deck of a drilling rig. Called Deepwater Horizon, the rig lay forty-eight miles off the Louisiana coast in the Gulf of Mexico. Designed to operate in waters 8,000 feet deep, the rig was 396 feet long and 256 feet wide. Dubbed a "floatel," it was a floating hotel, complete with sleeping quarters, laundry, kitchen, dining room, infirmary, movie theater, and a gymnasium with exercise machines.

Deepwater Horizon had been built in 2001 for Transocean, a

The Deepwater Horizon offshore drilling platform on fire.
(April 20, 2010)

Swiss firm, by South Korea's Hyundai Heavy Industries at a cost of $560 million. Transocean, in turn, leased the rig to British oil giant BP for $20,312 an *hour*. As with the *Exxon Valdez*, time was money. To save money, BP bosses ran Deepwater Horizon constantly. Drilling took priority over upkeep. "At nine years old, Deepwater Horizon has never been in drydock. We can only work around so much," a worker later told investigators. "Run it, break it, fix it," another man said. "That's how they work."

On April 20, Deepwater Horizon was operating in 5,000 feet of water. For days, crew members had noticed small blobs of oil floating on the surface nearby. This was nothing unusual, nothing to get excited about. Industry experts believe that about 1.4 million barrels of oil leak into the Gulf of Mexico each year from natural seeps, causing no damage to the environment.

But that night was different. Suddenly a giant bubble of natural gas shot up the drill pipe, sending a shower of mud into the air above the 242-foot derrick. The five-story-high, 450-ton blowout protector was supposed to prevent this sort of thing from happening. For some reason yet to be found, the device failed to do its job. Seconds later, the bubble itself burst from the well at high pressure, expanded, and exploded. "Oh, God. No!" Micah Sandell cried as the very air seemed to ignite. Thirty-five miles to the southwest, crew members aboard the rig Helix Q4000 saw an immense fireball climbing over the horizon.

Deepwater Horizon's crew had less than five minutes to scramble into the diesel-powered fiberglass lifeboats. Of the 126-man crew, 115, including Micah Sandell, escaped. The rest did not. Unable to reach the lifeboats in time, several jumped overboard. Since the platform was eighty feet high, each person struck the water with the same force as a car crashing into a stone wall at fifty-five miles an hour. Rescue crews never found the bodies of the jumpers; the bodies of the others probably went down with the flaming hulk when it sank on April 22.

During the following months, planners and work crews had to tackle two tasks at once: stop the oil leak and protect the environment.

The Deepwater Horizon spill was the largest in American history. Experts believe that 100,000 barrels (4.2 million gallons) of oil flowed into the Gulf of Mexico every day, totaling 4.9 million barrels (205.8 million gallons). This made it nearly nineteen times greater than the *Exxon Valdez* spill.

BP tried various methods to seal the runaway well. Among these was a "junk shot"—that is, clogging the blowout preventer by shooting shredded tires and golf balls into it under high pressure. The attempt failed. In July, engineers lowered a special iron cap and attached it to the broken pipe, sealing it and stopping the leak. Yet nobody could say whether, or how long, the cap would hold. "Killing" the well was the best solution. This involved drilling two relief wells to cut into the existing one at an angle, then pumping heavy drilling mud and cement down the hole. On September 19, the first relief well was completed. Workers then sealed the runaway well, officially killing it. Then they removed the blowout preventer so that engineers could figure out why it had failed.

Meanwhile, oil spewing from the broken well created a slick covering nearly 29,000 square miles, an area about the size of South Carolina. Checking the oil's spread was difficult, for ocean currents and winds drove it toward the coast. Thus, protecting the environment meant preventing the floating oil from spreading, diluting it, and removing whatever washed ashore.

From Texas to Florida, the Gulf Coast is one of the world's natural treasure-houses. Coastal wetlands, areas where the water level remains near or above ground level for much of the year, are nurseries for wildlife. Hundreds of species of fish, shellfish, turtles, and birds—such as gulls, pelicans, egrets, terns, herons—breed and feed in the wetlands.

Work crews fought on several fronts. Some set fire to oil patches floating in open water, keeping them from shore. Others placed floating booms—lines of inflated plastic barriers—parallel to the shoreline and built walls of sand onshore. Cleanup crews collected gobs of oil on the beaches, shoveling them into plastic bags, which they dumped in landfills. Finally, low-flying airplanes flew over oil slicks

A U.S. Air Force plane dropping oil-dispersing chemicals off the Deepwater Horizon spill. (May 5, 2010)

131

spraying dispersants, chemicals designed to break them up, allowing bacteria and evaporation to destroy them more easily. The problem is that dispersants are about 10,000 times deadlier to sea life than crude oil itself. Nobody knows how long these chemicals will stay active or what their long-term effects on sea life will be. "I think the imprint of the BP release, the discharge, will be detectable in the Gulf of Mexico for the rest of my life," ocean scientist Ian MacDonald told a congressional hearing on the spill. Sadly, he is probably right.

Hydrocarbons and Health

Man-made oil spills kill fish by the millions, while destroying their eggs by the trillions. Large spills often attract schools of fish, perhaps

Oil causes the feathers of waterbirds, like this cormorant, to stick together, taking away their ability to float and resist cold. (c. 1989)

132

because the fish mistake them for phytoplankton blooms. Oil smothers marine mammals—seals, walrus, sea otters, polar bears, small whales—by filling their nostrils and clogging their lungs. Swallowed, oil causes ulcers and stomach bleeding; it gets into eyes, leading to infections and blindness. It causes a seal's flippers to stick to its body, making it harder to swim and thus escape predators. It also masks the unique scent each seal pup and its mother rely upon to recognize the other. Since seal mothers nurse only their own pups, they reject their oil-covered pups. Oil plasters waterbirds' feathers together, making them lose their ability to resist cold and float. As a result, birds like penguins freeze to death or drown.

Oil affects human health in harmful ways, too. Oil and natural gas spills on land, from leaking pipelines, have harmed more people than any supertanker spill. The United States has two million miles of pipelines, enough to circle the globe eighty-eight times. Newspapers report that because of poor maintenance, pipeline leaks "are fouling the environment and causing fires and explosions that have killed more than 200 people and injured more than 1,000 in the past decade. And the numbers are increasing steadily."[1]

Automobiles have also taken a toll on health. In the early days of the auto, people praised gasoline because, unlike horses, it did not seem to pollute the air or the streets. It did, but there were so few autos that people hardly noticed the fumes. Nowadays, motor vehicles are far more numerous than horses ever were. (In 2005, there were 9.2 million horses in the United States, or one for every thirty-three people.) When burned in an engine, gasoline and oil leave wastes in the form of carbon particles, which form droplets of black soot. Should these get into your lungs, they can cause diseases like asthma, even cancer.

Children are highly sensitive to soot, possibly the chief cause of asthma among youngsters in the industrialized world. A medical researcher says:

Children whose developing lungs are particularly vulnerable suffer the most from air pollution. For children, breathing the air of cities with the worst pollution, such as Beijing, Calcutta, Mexico City, Shanghai, and Tehran, is the equivalent of smoking two packs of cigarettes a day.[2]

Equally important, life cannot exist on Earth without the so-called greenhouse gases. The name comes from the greenhouse, a glass building used for growing plants year-round. Light energy from the sun evaporates water in the greenhouse soil, which the glass walls and ceiling trap as vapor. Acting like the glass panes of a greenhouse, naturally occurring greenhouse gases, especially carbon dioxide, form an invisible barrier in the atmosphere. This is good. For by absorbing heat, the gases keep Earth warm enough to support life.

Yet there can be too much of a good thing. By driving motor vehicles, making electricity in coal-fired power plants, and heating our homes with oil, we release vast amounts of heat-trapping gases, particularly carbon dioxide, into the atmosphere. Added to the naturally occurring greenhouse gases, the man-made buildup results in global warming, a worldwide rise in temperature. Scientists estimate that, over the last 150 years, the burning of fossil fuels has increased the amount of carbon dioxide in Earth's atmosphere by 31 percent.

Most, but not all, scientists agree that global warming is changing rainfall patterns and increasing the severity of hurricanes. Global warming also threatens to spread tropical diseases, chiefly malaria, to once-cooler regions. Malaria, a disease carried by tropical mosquitoes, is the deadliest disease known to humanity. Since ancient times, it has killed more people than all wars, famines, and natural disasters combined. The World Health Organization reports:

> Malaria-carrying mosquitoes represent the clearest sign that global warming has begun to impact human health, [for] they are now found in cooler climates such as South Korea. . . . Warmer weather means that mosquitoes' breeding cycles are shortening, allowing them to multiply at a much faster rate, posing an even greater threat of disease.[3]

134

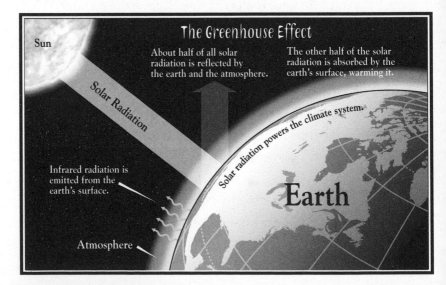

The Greenhouse Effect

Sun

About half of all solar radiation is reflected by the earth and the atmosphere.

The other half of the solar radiation is absorbed by the earth's surface, warming it.

Solar Radiation

Solar radiation powers the climate system.

Earth

Infrared radiation is emitted from the earth's surface.

Atmosphere

Melting of the ice caps at the North and South Poles due to global warming threatens to raise sea levels dangerously. Right now, for example, the Greenland ice cap is melting at a rate of more than forty-eight cubic *miles* each year! Should melting of the Greenland and polar ice caps continue at the present rate, coastal cities like New York and Shanghai, China, might become marshes, while Hawaii, Indonesia, the Philippines, and other island chains might be entirely swallowed by the Pacific Ocean.[4]

Climate change is also shrinking glaciers, those immense "rivers" of ice that slowly flow over land in the polar regions and high mountain valleys. Global warming could erase many glaciers in the Andes Mountains of South America within a generation, endangering over 100 million people. In Bolivia, the most glaring example, the mountain glaciers collect water in the short rainy season and release it for drinking, sanitation, and irrigation in the long dry season. But with warmer temperatures, they can no longer do so. A once-huge glacier, Chacaltya, disappeared in 2009. Villagers call another glacier, Illimani, "our God, our great protector." A decade ago, meltwater from Illimani enriched the farming villages in the valley below. Today the glacier is in retreat. "A lot of us think of not having kids anymore," says a local woman. "Without water or food, how would we survive? Why bring them here to suffer?"[5]

On the other hand, shifting ocean currents due to global warming might cool certain areas considerably. In some regions, this could lead to harsher winters and even make glaciers advance, as during the last ice age, 11,500 years ago. Back then, ice sheets up to three miles thick buried much of North America. No wonder former president Bill Clinton warns, "It's crazy for us to play with our children's future. We know what's happening to the climate, we have a highly predictable set of consequences if we continue to pour greenhouse gases into the atmosphere."[6]

Yet greenhouse gases and global warming are not the only dangers from fossil fuels. Take coal. It has always been a problem fuel. Each year, hundreds of miners die in underground accidents. Elevator failures send miners plummeting to the bottom of deep shafts. Tunnels cave in, burying miners. Naturally occurring poisonous gases, like methane, choke miners or explode, blowing them to bits.

Often coal companies go in for strip mining, because it is cheaper and easier than traditional mining. Instead of sinking deep shafts to reach the coal beds, they use giant bulldozers to knock down forests, scrape away the soil, and level mountaintops to reach coal beds closer to the surface. Appalachia, the region of the United States that includes the Appalachian Mountains, offers a stark example of strip mining. Jeff Biggers, an expert on the subject, points out that "an estimated 750,000 to 1 million acres of hardwood forests, a thousand miles of waterways and more than 470 mountains and their surrounding communities—an area the size of Delaware—have been erased from the southeastern mountain range in the last two decades. Thousands of tons of explosives—the equivalent of several Hiroshima atomic bombs—are set off in Appalachian communities every year."[7]

According to Greenpeace, a leading organization dedicated to preserving the natural environment, coal is "the dirtiest fuel there is."[8] Coal is jam-packed with poisons such as lead, arsenic, and mercury, a silver-colored metal. When released into the air through burning, mercury drifts back to Earth as particles of fine dust. Eventually, these particles accumulate in the bodies of animals, fish, and the humans who eat them. Mercury also finds its way into grains, fruits, and vegetables. Carbon dioxide emitted by burning coal is, of course, the chief greenhouse gas.

In 1997, the United States joined other nations to limit greenhouse gases from fossil fuels. Although diplomats signed an agreement, called the Kyoto Protocol (from the Japanese city of Kyoto, where it was drawn up), the Senate turned it down because it did not apply to newly industrialized countries. Chief among these countries is China, the world's leader in carbon dioxide emissions from coal. In 2007, China's coal-burning plants accounted for 21.4 percent of world emissions; the United States came in a close second at 19.9 percent.[9]

Finally, there is acid rain, a general term for rain, snow, hail, sleet, fog, or dew polluted by chemicals released by burning petroleum

Woods in the Jizera Mountains in the Czech Republic that have been damaged by acid rain. (c. 2006)

products and coal. Among these chemicals are sulfuric and nitric acids. Manufacturers use sulfuric acid to make automobile batteries, explosives, and paper. Nitric acid goes into fertilizers and explosives.

When these chemicals escape into the air, they combine with water vapor. Inevitably, they fall back to Earth as acid rain, harming the environment in many ways. For example, acid rain contaminates lakes, rivers, streams, forests, and soil, ruining crops. When it gets into water, it kills fish, frogs, turtles, and insects, including many insects that pollinate flowers, fruits, and vegetables. Unless pollinated by insects, many plants we rely upon for food will not grow. Acid rain harms forests by damaging the soil in which trees grow. Damaging the surface of leaves and needles makes it harder for trees to resist the cold, causing them to die. Acid rain also corrodes the metal frames of buildings and bridges so that they will collapse if not repaired.

The mercury in acid rain can taint everything we eat, drink, and breathe. For example, fish and shellfish—crab, crayfish, lobster, shrimp—contain nutrients that are important in a healthy diet. Nearly all, however, contain traces of mercury.

For most people, that is not a problem. Yet some fish and shellfish contain levels of mercury that may harm an unborn baby's or a young child's nervous system and even cause brain damage. One study shows that 630,000 children each year are exposed to possibly dangerous levels of mercury in their mother's womb. "In America," the study continues, "one in six children born every year have been exposed to mercury levels so high that they are potentially at risk for learning disabilities and motor skill impairment and short-term memory loss. That type of mercury exposure is caused by eating certain kinds of fish, which contain high levels of the toxin from natural and man-made sources such as emissions from coal-fired power plants."

138

In 2004, the Environmental Protection Agency urged women of childbearing age and young children not to eat fish known to contain high mercury levels: shark, swordfish, king mackerel, tilefish. California has ordered supermarkets and restaurants to warn customers about tuna for the same reason.[10]

Information on the effects of fossil fuels on the environment is constantly growing. Clearly, continued dependence on fossil fuels threatens our national security, as well as our economic, political, and physical well-being.

What to do?

IX

TOWARD
A NEW ENERGY ORDER

Energy independence will require an
all-hands-on-deck effort from America—effort from our
scientists and entrepreneurs; from businesses and from
every American citizen. . . . All of us will need to buy
more . . . fuel-efficient cars . . . and find new ways to
improve efficiency. . . . We can do this because we are
Americans. We do the improbable.

—Barack Obama, August 2008

Two Roads to Energy Independence

Two groups of energy experts offer solutions to the oil problem. One group hopes to end our addiction to foreign oil by making better use of existing fossil fuels, either alone or blended with other fuels. The other group calls for a new energy order—that is, giving up fossil fuels entirely, before the full effects of peak oil and climate change take firm hold. While both groups have offered many suggestions, some of those suggestions seem more practical than others.[1]

Yet all agree on this: no solution will come easily or cheaply. We may also be sure that there is no such thing as pure benefit. Every benefit has a downside. It carries a cost, often unexpected, but real enough. The most obvious is that to produce any form of energy, old or new, you need energy. Energy is also needed to extract the raw materials—iron, tin, copper, aluminum—to make devices you need to use the new energy. With this in mind, let's explore the leading solutions to the oil problem, realizing that none are perfect. For any solution has costs and problems that will keep it from being a cure-all.

Solutions Based on Fossil Fuels

Coal

Bring back coal, some experts urge. Coal is still the most abundant fossil fuel. The United States has the world's largest coal reserves, over 275 billion tons, enough to last 250 years if we use it at the same rate as today. Coal-fired power plants still produce 60 percent of the nation's electrical power.

However, coal mining uses vast amounts of oil. For example, digging machines burn as much as 100 gallons of oil an hour. As for the pollution created by burning coal, companies are working on ways to make "clean coal." A favorite way is to wash coal, thus removing some wastes before they can burn and travel up the smokestack. But washing results in poisonous sludge, black and thick as tar. Workers put the sludge in waste piles, much as sanitation workers once piled horse manure in vacant city lots. Rainwater filters through the piles, washing the poisons into streams and rivers. Eventually, they wind up in the sea, killing marine plants and animals.

Sometimes these wastes endanger entire communities. In December 2008, for example, 1.1 billion gallons of liquefied sludge burst through a dike next to a coal-fired power plant in Harriman, Tennessee. The foul-smelling gunk covered hundreds of acres of land and destroyed several homes. This accident released 100 times more poisonous materials, including mercury, than the *Exxon Valdez* oil spill. Public health officials are still not sure how much mercury remains in the soil, or how much of it has seeped into the local

A view of the Arctic National Wildlife Refuge. (c. 2005)

141

drinking-water supply. What is certain is that the accident left much of Harriman unfit for people to live in. So, for now, "clean coal" is a worthy goal, but not a practical reality. It may never be.[2]

Drilling for New Oil in the United States
Instead of coal, some urge Americans to "drill, baby, drill" for new sources of oil at home. An estimated ten billion barrels of oil lie under a 19.6-million-acre tract of land in the northeast corner of Alaska called the Arctic National Wildlife Refuge (ANWR). Unfortunately, oil from ANWR would be a drop in the bucket, and a mighty shallow bucket at that. For the place contains about the same amount of oil our country burns in little more than a year. ANWR is also home to roaming caribou herds; immense flocks of snow geese and other birds fly overhead during their fall migrations. Greenpeace and other groups concerned about the environment

fear that oil spills in ANWR will harm wildlife worse than even the *Exxon Valdez* disaster.[3]

Oil Shale and Oil Sands

Oil shale and oil sands were never buried deeply enough to generate the pressure and heat necessary for turning the remains of phytoplankton into liquid petroleum. These formations of sands really contain large amounts of bitumen mixed with clay and water. Both are low-energy fuels that, while found close to the surface, must be extracted at high cost by specialized equipment. Nevertheless, they have become attractive in a world demanding ever more energy. Geologists believe that the United States has 1.5 trillion barrels of oil locked up in the Green River shale deposits of Utah, Wyoming, and Colorado. Canada has another 1.7 trillion barrels of oil in its deposits of oil shale and oil sands.

142

Both, however, are extracted in ways harmful to the environment. Take oil sands. The Athabasca Valley in the province of Alberta, Canada, has the largest deposits of oil sands ever found, an area the size of North Carolina. Syncrude, Canada's leading producer, extracts the oil sand from surface mines less than 200 feet deep. To get at it, Syncrude strips away soil, destroying forests in the process. Once the oil sand is exposed, electric shovels five stories high claw it from the ground. A shovel's steel teeth, weighing one ton apiece, quickly wear out; welders must attach a new crown to each tooth every other day. (A photo demonstrating this process could not be provided as the producers of oil sand are resistant to the publication of images that depict their vehicles performing this destructive procedure.)

A shovel dumps its load, 400 tons at a time, into a supersized truck, which burns fifty gallons of diesel fuel an hour. An unbroken line of trucks takes the oil sand to an extraction plant, where boiling water washes the bitumen out of the sand. The energy to heat the water comes, mostly, from burning natural gas. Thus, critics accuse the oil-sands industry of wasting the cleanest fuel, natural gas, to make the dirtiest. Activists from Greenpeace once broke into an extraction plant to hoist a banner reading: "World's Dirtiest Oil: Stop the Tar Sands."

From the extraction plant, pipes carry the liquefied bitumen to a finishing plant to be made into synthetic crude oil. "Are we going to get serious about alternative energy?" asks Simon Dyer of the Pembina Institute, a Canadian environmental group. "The fact that we're willing to move four tons of earth for a single barrel [of synthetic crude oil] really shows that the world is running out of easy oil."[4]

It also shows the growing environmental cost of our oil addiction. Like "clean coal," synthetic crude oil leaves a deadly legacy. In making one barrel of synthetic crude oil, extraction and finishing plants leave behind two and a half barrels of wastewater, in effect a cocktail of toxic chemicals. The sticky, foul-smelling gunk is pumped into vast collecting ponds as large as fifty square miles in area. Wastewater ponds can easily become traps. In April 2008, for example, some 500 ducks apparently mistook the calm surface of an Alberta pond for a lake. After landing on the greasy surface, they were overcome by chemical fumes and died. Elsewhere, wastewater seeps into lakes and rivers, poisoning fish and underground streams that feed wells used for drinking water.

143

Natural Gas

Natural gas, we recall, is found along with oil or in fields of its own. We already use natural gas to heat our buildings, cook our food, and, along with coal, generate our electricity. It is the cleanest of all the fossil fuels. Burning it produces less carbon dioxide, the chief greenhouse gas, than burning coal or oil does. Motor vehicles powered by natural gas, such as the Honda Civic GX, do not harm the environment. It would be the perfect fuel, if only there were enough of it. Yet, as with oil, natural-gas production has peaked in the United States, and will probably do so in the rest of the world within a decade or two.[5]

Another problem: natural gas is difficult to get to market to sell. Producers cannot ship it in ordinary tankers because, as a gas, it expands so that small amounts fill large containers. The easiest way to ship natural gas overland is through special high-pressure pipelines that are expensive to build and keep in repair. Supercooled natural gas turns into a liquid. Shipped in tankers, liquefied natural gas (LNG) is highly explosive. In Cleveland, Ohio, in 1944, LNG leaked into the sewer system and exploded, killing 128 people. Large tanker ships filled with LNG are also tempting targets for terrorists. Blowing up an LNG tanker in a port city would cause terrific damage and loss of life.

Renewables: Key to the New Energy Order

Means and Ends

During the oil shock of 1973, Saudi Arabian oil minister Sheik Ahmed Yamani gave OPEC a stern warning. "If," he said, "we force western countries to invest heavily in finding alternative sources of energy, they will."[6] He was right. The triple threat of peak oil, high prices, and global warming has forced people to think about meeting their energy needs with renewable fuels instead of fossil fuels.

Though fossil fuels will eventually run out, renewables are just that: they naturally renew, or replace, themselves. While the sun shines, wind blows, and water flows, we can capture their energy. In effect, renewables are eternal and limitless. However, to use them with the best results, we must solve three tricky problems. First, we must capture their energy cheaply. Second, we must move that energy from where we collect it to where we use it. Finally, we must change that energy into easily available forms.

These tasks are easier to talk about than to achieve. For we cannot abandon fossil fuels no matter how much we may wish to or how hard we try—at least not right away. Like it or not, they have a role to play in the changeover to renewable energy. Fossil fuels buy us time. If used wisely, they can power the change before they become too scarce or run out. We need them to produce the raw materials for the machines that will make renewables, until these can make enough energy to do the job alone.

Biofuels

"Biofuel" refers to any fuel made from living things, particularly plants: farm crops, grasses, trees. Like phytoplankton, these contain stored energy from the sun, and more of them will always grow if they get sunlight. The most common biofuel is ethanol, a type of alcohol made from sugars found in grains such as corn, sugarcane, sugar beets, and

144

other plants. Motor vehicles can burn pure ethanol instead of gasoline. However, ethanol is usually a gasoline stretcher, something mixed with gasoline to make it go further. "Flex-fuel" vehicles are flexible; that is, they can run on either fuel. Ethanol keeps engines running smoothly and reduces air pollution but does not eliminate it.[7]

Americans favor ethanol made from corn, because they grow a lot of it in the Midwest. Yet corn ethanol is not an economical fuel. Farmers use large amounts of ammonia-based fertilizer, an oil product, to grow corn, and gasoline for planters, harvesters, and trucks to take their corn to market. Ethanol producers burn even more fossil fuels. A recent study by energy expert David Pimental of Cornell University shows that making ethanol from corn uses 29 percent more energy than the finished product yields. "There is just no energy benefit to using [plants] for liquid fuel," Pimental says. Worse, as growing corn for ethanol becomes more profitable, farmers will devote less land to

145

An ethanol-production plant beside a cornfield in South Dakota.

producing food. This, in turn, will raise food prices at a time when more than one billion people already live on the edge of starvation worldwide. If America decided to replace all gasoline with corn ethanol, it would have no land left to house, much less feed, the population![8]

Brazil, South America's largest country and the world's leading producer of ethanol from sugarcane, bans automobiles and light trucks that run on gasoline alone. It has replaced gasoline with pure sugar ethanol and blends of ethanol and gasoline. Despite sugar ethanol's advantages, its production has taken a heavy toll on the country's land and people.

Brazil once had dense rain forests covering about two-thirds of the country. Not anymore. Loggers have cut immense swaths, stripping the land of trees. Ranchers cut and burn forest land for pasture; big farming companies do the same to clear land. In 2001, satellite photos counted no fewer than 600 rain-forest fires burning on any given day. In the quarter century ending in 2005, man-made fires destroyed 211,180 square miles of Brazilian rain forest. This means that six football fields' worth of forest burn every minute.

Sugarcane is Brazil's most profitable crop. About one million people work on sugarcane plantations. These are among the country's poorest people. Cutting sugarcane is hard physical labor in a hot, humid climate. Eventually, it breaks the health of the strongest person. Journalist Jo Hartley, reporting on a study by the University of São Paulo, explains that "cane harvesters are able to work for an average of twelve years before their bodies are destroyed and they have to stop." Workers must each harvest 3.5 tons of sugarcane a day. To do this, they slash at the cane with a heavy steel blade called a machete 3,000 times a day.

Brazilian cane harvesters live as Iranian oil workers once lived at Abadan: in slums. Hartley continues: "There are numerous bedroom villages for the cane harvesters. These are groups of dirty huts thrown together in the oppressive heat. The huts are crude and the furnishings are stark. Children play in the dirt and raw sewage runs through nearby ditches."[9] Ethanol production, then, is beneficial for Brazil, but it does not benefit all Brazilians equally.

Thus, while corn ethanol and sugar ethanol have a role to play in the new energy order, they cannot create that order alone. Electricity seems the best way to end our addiction to oil and to meet our future energy needs. Though not a fuel itself, electricity is a form of energy that comes from something else. The electricity we need seems most likely to come from five sources: atoms, water, heat from within the earth, wind, and sunlight.

Nuclear Energy

Every object in the universe is made of atoms, invisible particles a million times smaller than a speck of dust. Nuclear energy is stored in

147

A cooling tower at the nuclear power station in Antwerp, Belgium.

an atom's nucleus, or core. Before scientists can make electricity, they must first release the energy from the core. The usual way of doing this is by splitting the atoms of uranium, a rare metal found in certain rocks. Scientists split atoms in a reactor, a machine designed for the purpose.

Reactors act like old-fashioned steam engines but do not burn wood or coal. Splitting atoms releases heat. Heat then boils water to form jets of high-pressure steam that strike a turbine. Turbines are windmill-like machines that turn; that is what "turbine" means. Fast-turning turbines drive generators, machines that generate, or make, electricity. In nuclear power plants, the leftover steam escapes into the air through giant cooling towers. Nuclear energy does not give off greenhouse gases.

Nuclear power plants make electricity for cities in many countries, including the United States. Nuclear reactors drive modern warships. A World War II submarine, we recall, had to surface often and run on its gasoline or diesel engines to recharge its electric batteries. Today's nuclear-powered submarines charge their batteries with small atom-splitting reactors. This allows a vessel to stay underwater for months, going around the world many times without having to surface for air. The reactor also powers machines that constantly take the air crew members exhale, purify it, and recirculate it. A nuclear submarine need only come to port to change crews and take food aboard. Modern aircraft carriers, like the USS *Theodore Roosevelt*, have nuclear reactors, too, only many times larger than a submarine's. Unlike any that served in World War II, today's nuclear-powered carriers can stay at sea for years without having to refuel.

But there are problems. Much of the energy used to mine uranium comes from fossil fuels. Nuclear wastes from spent (used-up) uranium are radioactive; that is, they give off harmful rays that can cause cancer and other serious illnesses. Unless power plants dispose of their reactor wastes properly, these can poison an area, making it unfit to live in for thousands of years. Nuclear power plants are scary things, too. People say that having them even miles away is like living with an atomic bomb in the backyard.

In 1979, we narrowly averted a nuclear disaster. A reactor in a plant at Three Mile Island, Pennsylvania, might have exploded had workers not acted quickly. The worst accident took place in April 1986 at Chernobyl in Ukraine, a country in Eastern Europe, then part of the Soviet Union. Radiation from an explosion and fire in the reactor poisoned food and water supplies for hundreds of miles around. Ukraine's government had to close the plant and force people to leave their homes, never to return. Even so, thousands have died of diseases linked to exposure to radiation. The countryside around Chernobyl is silent today, save for the twittering of birds and the flapping of loose shingles when the wind blows.

Advanced reactor designs, though not foolproof, are safer than ever before. Nuclear energy now provides 20 percent of the world's electricity. France gets over 75 percent of its electricity, more than any other country, from nuclear power.[10]

Despite human ingenuity, nature always has the final word. On March 11, 2011, an earthquake struck off Japan's northeastern coast, followed by a thirty-foot-high tsunami. The earthquake caused many injuries and sparked many fires. The tsunami washed away entire towns. At least 14,900 people died and another 9,800 were reported missing in the quake and resulting tsunami. An eyewitness described the aftermath:

> My first impression is that the man-made world has vomited
> up its innards. All that is normally hidden—the metal frames
> of buildings, piping, electric wires, and generators, as well as
> the crockery, bookshelves, televisions, and other bric-a-brac
> of modern living—is spewed into twisted view. Then there
> are the cars, mangled into shreds, on their back, on their
> side, and even the right way up, deposited as if by an
> invisible hand in the branches of a tree or the slope of a
> hillside. A few houses have survived, though most of those
> are tilted on their sides like drunkards. Many are hundreds
> of meters from where they once stood.[11]

The earthquake also damaged the Fukushima Dai-ichi nuclear plant on the coast, about 140 miles north of Tokyo. The shock cut electrical power to the water pumps that cool the reactor core and the pool where the spent fuel is stored. That, in turn, caused several explosions, allowing radioactive dust to get into the air. Fearing the worst, the Japanese government ordered more than 250,000 people to leave their homes near the site. Traces of radioactive iodine and other substances have been found in food and water supplies as far away as Tokyo, otherwise unaffected by the disaster. Japan faces not only the problem of rebuilding, but the long-term effects of the radiation released by Fukushima Dai-ichi. Only time will tell what, or how severe, these will be.[12]

Water Power

Nuclear power plants are not the only ones to use turbines and generators to make electricity. Other plants drive these machines with water, wind, sunlight, and heat from deep within the earth.

People have put the power of water to work since ancient times. Great paddle wheels, placed beside streams, turned stones that ground wheat into flour and drove saws that cut logs into beams for buildings and ships. In modern times, dams block rivers, forming reservoirs behind them. For example, Hoover Dam on the Colorado River, along the Nevada-Arizona border, is one of the largest structures ever built by humans. This mass of steel and concrete stands 726 feet high, 660 feet thick at the base, 48 feet thick at the top, and 1,244 feet long. When the reservoir gates open, water from Lake Mead rushes through pipes to turbines. These drive generators to create hydroelectric power—that is, electric power from water. Power lines leading from the generators supply much of the electricity used in Arizona, Nevada, and Southern California, including the city of Los Angeles.

The same principle applies to creating electricity from ocean tides and waves. America has 12,383 miles of coastline along the Atlantic, Pacific, and Arctic oceans. Water rushing into giant steel and concrete containers, then rushing out again, drives turbines and generators. Making electricity from tides and waves is still experimental, for scientists have yet to learn how to keep the force of the water from destroying the containers.

150

The hydroelectric power generated by the Hoover Dam supplies much of the electricity used in Arizona, Nevada, and Southern California. (c. 1940–1960)

Geothermal Energy

The word "geothermal" comes from two Greek words: *geo* (for "earth") and *therme* (for "heat"). Geothermal energy, then, is heat from within the earth. "The heat of the earth is there; you can bank on it," says scientist Steven Chu, former head of the Lawrence Berkeley National Laboratory.[13]

Geothermal energy is renewable, because rainwater and melted snow that sink into the ground collect in deep reservoirs. Earth's crust, we recall, is like an eggshell broken into ever-moving slabs called plates. These plates are so heavy, each weighing trillions of tons, that their pressure heats underground water, turning it into steam. So does heat from Earth's core.

Geysers, like Old Faithful in Yellowstone National Park, demonstrate geothermal energy by spouting steam and boiling water into the air. (c. 2005)

152

Steam finds its way to the surface in much the same way as an oil seep, through cracks in the crust, emerging as hot springs and geysers. Hot springs may flow steadily or become mud pots, pools of bubbling mud. Geysers shoot columns of steam and boiling water into the air, sometimes 120 feet or more. America's most famous geyser, Old Faithful in Yellowstone National Park, Wyoming, erupts every hour or so. Most of our hot-water reservoirs are in the western states of Alaska and Hawaii. These lie in areas where two plates rub against each other. Earthquakes and volcanoes develop along these plate lines, too.

We already use limited amounts of geothermal energy to heat buildings and make electricity. In making electricity, a well drilled into an underground reservoir carries boiling water and steam to a turbine, which powers a generator. After the steam condenses, other pipes return the water to the reservoir. Geothermal energy produces electricity cheaply. Yet steam from underground water may contain harsh chemicals that ruin turbines and, if released into the air, spread pollution. Another problem: drilling deep wells to get at the hot water can be dangerous. An experimental well in Switzerland set off a string of minor earthquakes.

Wind Power

153

Wind is air in motion. The sun's rays heat the earth's surface unevenly. As the air above warmer areas expands and rises, cooler air flows in to replace it, creating wind. Wind is everlasting; it will blow as long as the sun shines.

Wind turbines are modern versions of windmills made of metal

A wind farm near Tehachapi, California.

instead of wood and canvas. Today's high-tech turbines are giants, standing up to 410 feet tall, or about the height of a twenty-story building, and have three propeller-like blades. These blades are up to 148 feet in length, roughly the wingspan of a jumbo jet airliner. The wind causes turbine blades to spin, turning a generator to produce electricity.

Groups of wind power plants, or wind farms, are built where the wind blows strongly and steadily. Energy experts have called America the Saudi Arabia of wind power. This is no exaggeration. Wind farms, each with dozens of machines, dot the Great Plains, the Midwest, and the waters off the Atlantic coast. Since no hills or trees block them, Great Plains winds may reach 100 miles an hour, a speed seen only at the seashore or during a tornado.

In one year, a single wind turbine can produce as much energy as 12,000 barrels of oil. The 421 turbines at the Horse Hollow Wind Energy Center in Texas, the world's largest wind farm, can meet the energy needs of 200,000 homes a year. The use of wind-generated electricity is growing rapidly. Wind is an ideal energy source. Not only is it free, it is (supposedly) harmless to the environment. Turbines produce no air or water pollution, because they burn no fossil fuel.

Yet turbines can pose a serious threat to wildlife. Location is everything. In some places, scientists believe, house cats kill ten birds for every one killed by a turbine. Elsewhere, in places like Altamont, a fifty-square-mile site in the Diablo Mountains east of San Francisco, California, they are mass killers; some environmentalists call them "toilet brushes in the sky." Altamont is the nation's second largest turbine facility. However, it lies on a major bird migration route. For years, the "massive fiberglass blades on more than 4,000 windmills have been chopping up tens of thousands of birds that fly into them, including golden eagles, red-tailed hawks, burrowing owls and other raptors [birds of prey]." Another study finds that beaked whales, creatures the size of a rhinoceros, get confused by offshore turbines, leading them to come up on the beach, where they die. Moreover, to make a wind turbine, you need oil or coal to power the machines that dig the mines and move and process the materials that form these devices.[14]

Solar Energy

We know that the light and heat produced by the sun sustain life on Earth. Every plant and animal, from the tiniest plankton to the biggest whale, owes its existence to the sun. Solar energy may also offer the best cure for our fossil-fuel addiction. Enough energy reaches Earth in forty minutes to meet all the world's needs for a year! Using just a fraction of this could provide all the electricity America uses, with plenty to spare.

People have used solar energy since the dawn of history. The ancient Greeks and Chinese made burning mirrors, large pieces of glass, to focus sun rays to start fires. Archimedes, a Greek mathematician and engineer, built devices to defend Syracuse, a city on the southern coast of Sicily, an island in the Mediterranean Sea, against the Roman

155

The Nellis Solar Power Plant in Clark County, Nevada. (c. 2005)

navy. Among these devices were cranes designed to lift ships out of the water, then send them crashing to Earth. Legend has it that Archimedes used curved U-shaped bronze shields, polished to a high shine, to focus sunlight on ships' sails, setting them on fire.

Modern burning mirrors, called solar panels, are like Archimedes's shields, only made of steel, glass, and plastic. Tilted toward the sun, they focus light on copper water pipes. The boiling water makes steam to drive a turbine attached to an electric generator. Like wind power, solar power is free, clean, and unlimited. It produces no air or water pollution.

Germany leads the world in generating electricity from solar energy. While still far behind Germany, America is beginning to take solar energy seriously. In 2007, about 1 percent of the nation's electricity came from solar power; by 2025, it is expected to reach 10 percent. Twelve cities, among them Philadelphia, Denver, and Houston, have major solar energy projects. Solar power plants in California provide enough electricity for a community of 350,000 people for one year. Homeowners across the nation mount solar panels on their roofs; these provide enough power for warmth, cooking, and hot water. Devices called solar cells change light directly into electricity. Solar cells power small things like watches, calculators, and lighted road signs.

In the United States, the National Aeronautics and Space Administration (NASA) has experimented with solar-powered aircraft since the mid-1990s. One model, the *Helios* (Greek for "sun"), is basically a wing covered with solar panels that generate the energy to drive its twelve propellers. This aircraft has no onboard human pilot, but is remotely controlled from the ground. *Helios* can stay aloft for weeks, even months, flying slowly, between fifteen and twenty-five miles an hour, at an altitude of nearly 97,000 feet. At night, a backup battery system, which stores energy during the day, enables *Helios* to keep flying until sunrise. Eventually, solar-powered machines may replace the aircraft we are familiar with today. That would be a good thing, for jet aircraft use kerosene-based fuel.

Some Thoughts at the End

There is no single, quick, or cheap solution to our fossil-fuel problem. No form of renewable energy is perfect. It seems, then, that the answer lies in using a *combination* of sources, from water and geothermal to nuclear, wind, and solar—and yes, even some biofuels. Nature is guided by its own laws, not by human wants and needs. Not every place is blessed with renewable energy resources. Even where abundant, they are not always reliable. Ocean tides vary in strength, depending on the season. Wind dies down, even at the seashore. Clouds and night hide the sun. Yet in each case, we may be able to store the energy until the source becomes available again.

Electricity seems like our best hope, but making it is only the first step on a long road. Electricity, however it is made, must travel from the source to the consumer over a power grid—that is, a network of overhead wires and underground cables. Engineers designed America's existing power grids for plants that made electricity by burning coal, oil, or natural gas to boil water for turbines and generators. Today these grids are aging, fragile, and unreliable. Occasionally a section of a grid breaks down, cutting power and plunging entire regions into darkness. We need a unified power grid, one that can move the "new" electricity from any source to any place, cheaply and safely.

Building a modern power grid will take decades and hundreds of billions of dollars. How to pay for it? Meanwhile, we must design motor vehicles than can run on electricity, another job demanding time and money. These vehicles will require plug-in outlets, millions of them, everywhere, to recharge batteries.

Power plants, however, produce only electricity, not the other products made from oil, such as plastics and fertilizers. Scientists must find substitutes for these products, or we must learn to get along without them.

Yet we have no choice. Time is running out. A report by the Institute for the Analysis of Global Security, a Washington think tank, goes to the heart of the problem. Although the report deals with oil,

157

Overhead wires, like these, and underground cables form the power grid that delivers electricity to Americans throughout the country.

158

its conclusion applies to natural gas and coal as well: "It is in our best interest to . . . embark on a revolutionary change that will lead us away from oil dependency rather than drag our feet and suffer the [costs] of becoming growingly dependent on a diminishing resource."[15]

Truer words were never written.

Notes

II BLACK GOLD

1. Book of Daniel, chapter 3.

2. Daniel Yergin, *The Prize: The Epic Quest for Oil, Money, and Power*, New York: Simon & Schuster, 1991, 57.

3. Zayn Bilkadi, "The Oil Weapons," *Saudi Aramco World*, January/February 1995, www.saudiaramcoworld.com.issue/1999501/the.oil.weapons.htm.

4. Bilkadi, "The Oil Weapons."

5. Heather Pringle, *The Mummy Congress: Science, Obsession, and the Everlasting Dead*, New York: Hyperion, 2001, 46.

6. "The History of Greek Fire," http://stronghold.heavengames.com/sc/history/greekfire.

7. Laurence Bergreen, *Marco Polo: From Venice to Xanadu*, New York: Alfred A. Knopf, 2007, 156.

8. Yergin, *The Prize*, 29–30.

9. Burton W. Folsom Jr., "John D. Rockefeller and the Oil Industry," *The Freeman*, October 1988, www.thefreemanonline.org/columns/john-d-rockefeller-and-the-oil-industry.

10. Folsom, "John D. Rockefeller and the Oil Industry."

11. Peter Collier and David Horowitz, *The Rockefellers: An American Dynasty*, New York: Holt, Rinehart and Winston, 1976, 231.

12. Yergin, *The Prize*, 39.

13. Collier and Horowitz, *The Rockefellers*, 19.

14. Yergin, *The Prize*, 79.

15. Ron Chernow, *Titan: The Life of John D. Rockefeller, Sr.*, New York: Random House, 1998, 101.

16. Yergin, *The Prize*, 104.

III THE DESTINY OF NATIONS

1. Allan Anderson, *Roughnecks & Wildcatters*, Ottawa, ON: Macmillan of Canada, 1981, 13.

2. Anderson, *Roughnecks & Wildcatters*, 29.

3. "Hero of Spindletop," *Time*, June 20, 1955.

4. "How Much Oil Did Spindletop Produce?," http://library.thinkquest.org/J0112442
/produce.html. See also Robert Wooster and Christine Moor Sanders, "Spindletop Oilfield,"
The Handbook of Texas Online, www.tshaonline.org/handbook/online/articles/dos3; and
Robert McDaniel and Henry Dethloff, *Pattillo Higgins and the Search for Texas Oil*, College
Station: Texas A&M University Press, 1989.

5. Anderson, *Roughnecks & Wildcatters*, 12.

6. Anderson, *Roughnecks & Wildcatters*, 2.

7. Anderson, *Roughnecks & Wildcatters*, 36.

8. Anderson, *Roughnecks & Wildcatters*, 32.

9. Winston S. Churchill, *The World Crisis*, New York: Charles Scribner's Sons, 1951, 134.

10. Stephen Kinzer, *All the Shah's Men: An American Coup and the Roots of Middle East Terror*,
Hoboken, NJ: John Wiley & Sons, 2003, 47.

11. Kinzer, *All the Shah's Men*, 48.

12. Kinzer, *All the Shah's Men*, 38.

13. Kinzer, *All the Shah's Men*, 39.

14. John Ellis, *Eye-Deep in Hell: Trench Warfare in World War I*, New York: Pantheon Books, 1976, 5.

15. Yergin, *The Prize*, 177, 813.

16. Yergin, *The Prize*, 183.

IV AUTOMOBILES AND MIDDLE EASTERN OIL

1. Richard Heinberg, *The Party's Over: Oil, War and the Fate of Industrial Societies*, Gabriola, BC:
New Society Publishers, 2003, 67.

2. Nathan Miller, *New World Coming: The 1920s and the Making of Modern America*, New York:
Scribner, 2003, 181.

3. James J. Flink, *The Automobile Age*, Cambridge, MA: MIT Press, 1988, 43.

4. Eric Morris, "From Horse Power to Horsepower," *Access*, Spring 2007,
www.uctc.net/access/30/Access%2030%20-%2002%20-%20Horse%20Power.pdf.

5. Joel A. Tarr, "Urban Pollution—Many Long Years Ago," *American Heritage*; Stephen Davies,
"The Great Horse Manure Crisis of 1894," *The Freeman*, September 2004.

6. James J. Flink, *The Car Culture*, Cambridge, MA: MIT Press, 1975, 39.

7. Yergin, *The Prize*, 210.

8. "The Proclamation of Baghdad," *Harper's Magazine*, May 2003, www.harpers.org
/archive/2003/05/0079593.

9. David Fromkin, *A Peace to End All Peace: The Fall of the Ottoman Empire and the Creation of the
Modern Middle East*, New York: Avon Books, 1990, 508.

10. David Omissi, "Baghdad and British Bombers," *The Guardian*, January 19, 1991,
www.globalpolicy.org/component/content/article/169/36388.html.

11. Margaret MacMillan, *Peacemakers: The Paris Conference of 1919 and Its Attempt to End War*, London: John Murray, 2001, 409.

12. Yergin, *The Prize*, 204.

13. David Holden and Richard Johns, *The House of Saud: The Rise and Rule of the Most Powerful Dynasty in the Arab World*, New York: Holt, Rinehart and Winston, 1981, 64.

14. Holden and Johns, *The House of Saud*, 70.

15. Holden and Johns, *The House of Saud*, 69.

16. Michael B. Oren, *Power, Faith, and Fantasy: America in the Middle East, 1776 to the Present*, New York: W. W. Norton, 2007, 411.

17. Jane Waldron Grutz, "Prelude to Discovery," *Saudi Aramco World*, January/February 1999, www.saudiaramcoworld.com/issue/199901/prelude.to.discovery.htm; Yergin, *The Prize*, 287.

18. Oren, *Power, Faith, and Fantasy*, 414.

19. Yergin, *The Prize*, 300–301; Oren, *Power, Faith, and Fantasy*, 415; Karl E. Meyer and Shareen Blair Brysac, *Kingmakers: The Invention of the Modern Middle East*, New York: W. W. Norton, 2008, 254.

20. Yergin, *The Prize*, 183.

V HOPELESS MONSTERS

1. William H. Herndon and Jesse W. Weik, *Abraham Lincoln: The True Story of a Great Life*, New York: D. Appleton, 1902, II, 148.

2. Robert G. L. Waite, *The Psychopathic God: Adolf Hitler*, New York: Basic Books, 1977, 77.

3. Robert Goralski and Russell W. Freeburg, *Oil and War: How the Deadly Struggle for Fuel in World War II Meant Victory or Defeat*, New York: William Morrow, 1987, 53.

4. Goralski and Freeburg, *Oil and War*, 61.

5. Goralski and Freeburg, *Oil and War*, 93.

6. Yergin, *The Prize*, 319.

7. Goralski and Freeburg, *Oil and War*, 106.

8. Winston Groom, *1942: The Year That Tried Men's Souls*, New York: Atlantic Monthly Press, 2005, 161.

9. Goralski and Freeburg, *Oil and War*, 165.

10. Richard Overy, *Why the Allies Won*, New York: W. W. Norton, 1995, 234.

11. Yergin, *The Prize*, 346; *The United States Strategic Bombing Survey, Summary Report (European War)*, September 30, 1945, www.absoluteastronomy.com/topics/Strategic_bombing_survey_(Europe).

12. Yergin, *The Prize*, 387.

13. Yergin, *The Prize*, 358.

14. Goralski and Freeburg, *Oil and War*, 313.

15. Goralski and Freeburg, *Oil and War*, 324.

VI RICHEST PRIZE, GREATEST PROBLEM

1. Sonia Shah, *Crude: The Story of Oil*, New York: Seven Stories Press, 2004, 12.

2. Richard C. Duncan, "The Peak of World Oil Production and the Road to the Olduvai Gorge," www.hubbertpeak.com/duncan/road2olduvai.pdf.

3. Yergin, *The Prize*, 485.

4. Yergin, *The Prize*, 487.

5. "Israel 1948–1967: Six Day War Background," http://palestinefacts.org/pf_1948to1967_sixday_backgd .php.

6. John Loftus and Mark Aarons, *The Secret War Against the Jews: How Western Espionage Betrayed the Jewish People*, New York: St. Martin's Press, 1994, 47.

7. Yergin, *The Prize*, 617.

8. Owen Bowcott, "UK Feared Americans Would Invade Gulf During 1973 Oil Crisis," *The Guardian*, January 1, 2004, www.guardian.co.uk/politics/2004/jan/01/uk.past3.

9. Kinzer, *All the Shah's Men*, 50, 67.

10. Kinzer, *All the Shah's Men*, 124.

11. Meyer and Brysac, *Kingmakers*, 324.

12. *Public Papers 1977*, vol. 2, Washington, DC: Government Printing Office, 2221.

13. Efraim Karsh, *The Iran-Iraq War, 1980–1988*, Oxford: Osprey Publishing, 2002. See also Ian Brown, *Khomeini's Forgotten Sons: The Story of Iran's Boy Soldiers*, London: Grey Seal, 1990.

14. Yergin, *The Prize*, 710; Karsh, *Iran-Iraq War*, 39, 63.

15. Dilip Hiro, *Blood of the Earth: The Battle for the World's Vanishing Oil Resources*, New York: Nation Books, 2007, 122.

16. Patrick Tyler, *A World of Trouble: The White House and the Middle East—from the Cold War to the War on Terror*, New York: Farrar, Straus & Giroux, 2009, 337–338; Human Rights Watch, "Genocide in Iraq: The Anfal Campaign Against the Kurds," www.hrw.org/legacy/reports/1993/iraqanfal/.

17. James A. Paul, "Oil Companies in Iraq: A Century of Rivalry and War," Global Policy Forum, November 2003, www.globalpolicy.org/security/oil/2003/2003companiesiniraq.htm.

18. Peter Dale Scott, "Bush's Deep Reasons for War on Iraq," http://socrates.berkeley.edu /~pdscott/iraq.html; Derrick Z. Jackson, "Big Oil and the War in Iraq," *The Boston Globe*, June 24, 2008, www.boston.com/bostonglobe/editorial_opinion/oped/articles/2008/06/24/big_oil_and_the_war _in_iraq/.

19. Bob Woodward, "Greenspan: Ouster of Hussein Crucial for Oil Security," *The Washington Post*, September 17, 2007, www.washingtonpost.com/wp-dyn/content/article/2007/09 /16/AR2007091601287.html.

20. Paul, "Oil Companies in Iraq."

21. Lutz Kleveman, "Oil and the New Great Game," *The Nation*, February 16, 2004, www.thirdworldtraveler.com/Oil.

VII A DAY OF RECKONING

1. Shah, *Crude,* 34.

2. Shah, *Crude,* 38; John Carey, "The Real Question: Should Oil Be Cheap?" *Business Week,* August 4, 2008, www.businessweek.com/magazine/content/08_31/b4094000658012.htm.

3. John Vidal, "The End of Oil Is Closer Than You Think," *The Guardian,* April 21, 2005, www.guardian.co.uk/science/2005/apr/21/oilandpetrol.news.

4. Duncan, "The Peak of World Oil Production."

5. Shah, *Crude,* 39; Kleveman, "Oil and the New Great Game"; "Fast Facts About Fossil Fuels," www.umich.edu/~envst320/fossil/html.

6. Shah, *Crude,* 144, 155; Robert Bryce, "Oil for War," *The American Conservative,* March 10, 2008, http://www.amconmag.com/article/2008/mar/10/00006/.

7. R. James Woolsey, "Defeating the Oil Weapon," *Commentary,* September 2002, www.commentarymagazine.com/viewarticle.cfm/defeating-the-oil-weapon-9497.

VIII FOSSIL FUELS AND THE NATURAL ENVIRONMENT

1. Jeff Nesmith and Ralph K. M. Haurwitz, "Spills and Explosions Reveal Lax Regulation of Powerful Industry," *Austin American-Statesman,* July 22, 2001, www.mail-archive.com/sustainablelorgbiofuel@sustainablelists.org/msg07695.html.

2. Lester R. Brown, Michael Renner, and Brian Halweil, *Vital Signs 1999: The Environmental Trends That Are Shaping Our Future,* New York: W. W. Norton, 1999, 165.

3. Hrvoje Hranjski, "WHO: Climate Change Threatens Millions," Associated Press, April 7, 2008, www.climateark.org/shared/reader/welcome.aspx?linkid=96415.

4. John Roach, "Greenland Ice Sheet Is Melting Faster, Study Says," *National Geographic News,* August 10, 2006, news.nationalgeographic.com/news/2006/08/060810-greenland.html.

5. Elisabeth Rosenthal, "In Bolivia, Water and Ice Tell of Climate Change," *The New York Times,* December 14, 2009, www.nytimes.com/2009/12/14/science/earth/14bolivia.html.

6. Bill Clinton at the United Nations Climate Conference, Montreal, December 9, 2005, http://channah.blog.ca/2005/12/10/Clinton_Montreal-374670.

7. Jeff Biggers, "'Clean' Coal? Don't Try to Shovel That," *The Washington Post,* March 2, 2008, www.washingtonpost.com/wp-dyn/content/article/2008/02/29/AR2008022903390.html.

8. Greenpeace, "Unmasking the Truth Behind 'Clean Coal,'" www.greenpeace.org/seasia/en/campaigns/climate-change/climate-impacts/coal/the-clean-coal-myth.

9. "Big Hitters, Big Emitters," *Financial Times,* December 9, 2009.

10. Public Broadcasting Service, "The Mercury Story," January 21, 2005, www.pbs.org/now/science/mercuryinfish.html; Environmental Protection Agency, U.S. Food and Drug Administration, "What You Need to Know About Mercury in Fish and Shellfish," March 2004 (updated November 23, 2009), www.fda.gov/Food/ResourcesForYou/Consumers/ucm110591.htm.

IX TOWARD A NEW ENERGY ORDER

1. Kenneth S. Deffeyes, *Beyond Oil: The View from Hubbert's Peak*, New York: Hill & Wang, 2005, 113; Duncan, "The Peak of World Oil Production"; Heinberg, *The Party's Over*, 111–112; Shah, *Crude*, 148–149.

2. Bryan Walsh, "Exposing the Myth of Clean Coal Power," *Time*, January 10, 2009, www.time.com/time/health/article/0,8599,1870599,00.html.

3. Duncan, "The Peak of World Oil Production."

4. Robert Kunzig, "The Canadian Oil Boom," *National Geographic*, March 2009, 34–59.

5. Deffeyes, *Beyond Oil*, 53; Shah, *Crude*, 169–170; Natural Gas Supply Association, "Natural Gas and the Environment," http://naturalgas.org/environment/naturalgas.asp.

6. Shah, *Crude*, 160.

7. Department of Energy, "Ethanol Made from Corn and Other Crops," http://tonto.eia.doe.gov/kids/energy.cfm?page=biofuel_home-basics.

8. Larry West, "The Pros and Cons of Biofuels," http://environment.about.com/od/fossilfuels/a/biofuels.htm; Heinberg, *The Party's Over*, 155.

9. Jo Hartley, "The High Price of Cheap Ethanol in Brazil," *Natural News*, February 2, 2009, www.naturalnews.com/025505_ethanol_Brazil_fuel.html.

10. Hiro, *Blood of the Earth*, 245–255.

11. Alice Park, "Feeding on Fallout: Radiation May Persist for Years in Japan's Food Chain and Water Supply," *Time*, April 2, 2011.

12. David Pilling, "The Aftermath," *Financial Times Weekend*, March 26–27, 2011.

13. Matthew L. Wald, "The Power of Renewables," *Scientific American*, March 2009, 56–61.

14. John Ritter, "Wind Turbines Taking Toll on Birds of Prey," *USA Today*, January 4, 2005, www.usatoday.com'news/.../21005-01-04-windmills-usat-x.htm.

15. Institute for the Analysis of Global Security, "The Future of Oil," www.iags.org/futureofoil.html.

Some Words to Remember

ANTHRACITE The hardest type of coal.

ASPHALT A sticky, nearly solid form of oil, commonly used to pave roads.

BITUMINOUS COAL A semi-hard type of coal that gives off lots of heat and smoke when burned. The most plentiful and widely used type of coal in the United States.

BLOWOUT An uncontrolled release of crude oil or natural gas from an oil or natural-gas well. Also called an oil gusher, gusher, or wild well.

BLOWOUT PREVENTER A series of valves used to slow and to stop an uncontrolled escape of crude oil or natural gas.

BOREHOLE The hole made by a drill bit. Also called a wellbore.

CAP ROCK A harder type of rock overlaying a softer or weaker type of rock, such as reservoir rock.

CARBON The chief chemical element in coal, oil, and diamonds; the basic building block of life on Earth, found in all plants and animals. In scientific terms, we humans are simply carbon-based creatures.

CASING Steel lining used to prevent caving in of the sides of an oil well.

CEMENT A mixture of sand, gravel, and binding compound that hardens as it dries. Used to keep the casing in place in an oil well.

CHRISTMAS TREE A group of safety valves used to control the flow of crude oil and natural gas. Also called a "blowout preventer."

COAL A solid, carbon-rich substance formed by dead plant matter buried within the earth and pressed together for millions of years, commonly used as fuel.

CONCESSION A license given by a country to a foreign citizen or company to produce or sell a given product or service free of competition.

CRUDE OIL Unrefined petroleum as it comes from reservoir rock beneath the earth's surface.

DRILL BIT The cutting head used for boring oil wells.

DRILL STRING Lengths of steel pipe joined, one behind the other, and tipped by a drill bit.

DRILLING MUD A mixture of water and chemicals used to cool a spinning drill bit and force rock cuttings to the surface through the space between the drill string and wall of the borehole.

FOSSIL FUEL A fuel, such as coal, oil, or natural gas, formed from the carbon-rich remains of prehistoric plants.

FRACTIONAL DISTILLATION The process of separating different ingredients (fractions) of crude oil by boiling and then collecting them as the vapors cool at different temperatures in a fractionating tower.

GLOBAL WARMING The worldwide warming of Earth due to the buildup in the atmosphere of gases, particularly carbon dioxide, from the burning of fossil fuels.

GREENHOUSE GASES Carbon dioxide and other gases, occurring naturally or given off by burning fossil fuels, which form a layer in the atmosphere that warms the earth. *See* **global warming.**

HYDROCARBON A combination of the elements hydrogen and carbon.

KEROGEN A carbon-rich material formed from the decaying remains of plants.

KEROSENE A flammable liquid made from the fractional distillation of crude oil.

LIGNITE A type of coal that contains visible remains of plants and gives off little heat and lots of smoke when burned. Also called brown coal.

NATURAL GAS A gas formed beneath the earth's surface, often together with, or near, oil deposits.

OIL-GAS WINDOW A depth beneath the earth's surface, ranging from 7,500 to 15,000 feet, at which pressure and heat cause chemical changes that turn kerogen into oil and natural gas.

PEAT A soggy mass of dead, decaying plant matter; the first stage in coal formation.

PETROCHEMICALS Chemicals made from petroleum or natural gas.

PHOTOSYNTHESIS The chemical process by which green plants use the energy from sunlight to turn carbon dioxide and water into food, giving off oxygen as a by-product.

REFINERY A special type of factory that purifies (refines) crude oil into various petrochemicals.

RESERVOIR ROCK A layer of rock containing microscopic holes, or pores, where oil and natural gas accumulate. *See* **cap rock.**

SEEP A place where crude oil reaches Earth's surface through cracks in reservoir rocks.

SOURCE ROCK Layers of rock in which kerogen turns to crude oil or natural gas.

Image Credits

Index

Page references in *italics* refer to illustrations.

World War II and, 81

B

Baba Gurgur, Iraq, 61
bacteria
    decay and, 4
    decomposition of oil, 11
    phytoplankton and, 8
Baghdad, Iraq, 13, 56, 57, 59, 99
Bahrain, oil industry in, 61–63, 68
Baku oil fields, Russia, 42–43, 73, 75
Bartlett, Albert, 93
battleships, 39–42, *42*, 46, 48, 85–86, 89
Beaumont, Texas, 36–37
Bedouins, 59, 63, 65, 66, 68
Belgium
    nuclear power station in Antwerp, *147*
    World War I and, 45
    World War II and, 74, 81
Bell, Gertrude, 64–65
Bible, 12
Biggers, Jeff, 136
Big Inch pipeline, 80, *80*
bin Laden, Osama, 114–115, *114*
biofuels, 144–147, 157
bitumen, 142–143
bituminous coal
    defined, 166
    formation of, 6
black gangs, 39–40
Black Giant oil field, 56, 118
"black gold," as nickname for crude oil, 1
blitzkrieg (lightning war), *72*, 73, 74, 76, 82
blowout preventer
    Deepwater Horizon disaster and, 129, 130
    defined, 166
    oil well drilling and, 35–36
blowouts
    defined, 166
    oil well drilling and, 35–36
    release of crude oil or natural gas, 10
Bolivia, 135
The Book of the Powers of Remedies, 12
borehole, defined, 166
Brazil, 146
British Malaya, 76
British Petroleum (BP), 105, 127, 129, 130
Brotherhood (Ikhwan), 65–66

Brown, John, 19
Bulgaria, 45
Bush, George H. W., 112
Bush, George W., 115

C

California
    gold rush of, 21
    La Brea Tar Pits, 11–12, *11*
    mercury in fish and, 138
    oil industry in, 56, 118
    solar energy and, 156
    wind farms and, *153*, 154
Canada, 56, 142–143
cap rock
    defined, 166
    oil or gas reservoirs under, 10, 33
carbon
    in automobile fumes, 133
    coal and, 6, 18
    crude oil and, 8–9, 116
    defined, 166
    diamond as form of, 33
    kerogen and, 8
carbon dioxide, 133, 134, 136, 143
Carboniferous Period, 5
carnivores, 4
Carter, Jimmy, 106–107
casings
    defined, 166
    oil well drilling and, 34
Caspian Sea, 116
cement
    casings and, 34
    defined, 166
    oil wells plugged with, 69, 130
    shale and, 8
Central Intelligence Agency (CIA), 104–106, 109
Chacaltya glacier, 135
change
    climate change, 134–135, 139
    as key rule of science, 2
Chernobyl nuclear accident, 149
Chevron, 98
China, 16, 19–20, 75, 123, 136, 155
Christmas tree
    defined, 166

earthquakes, 3, 149

East Jerusalem, 99

ecoterrorism, of Saddam Hussein, 112, 127

Eden, Anthony, 97

Edison, Thomas A., 27, *28*

Egypt
    as British colony, 40
    British occupation of, 95
    historical use of oil in, 13
    Israel and, 98–99, 100
    Suez Canal and, 95, 96–98

Eisenhower, Dwight D., 104

electricity
    for automobiles, 51
    coal-fired power plants and, 134, 140
    geothermal energy and, 151–153
    for lighting, 27, 50
    natural gas and, 143
    nuclear energy and, 147–150
    solar energy and, 155–156
    as solution to energy problems, 146–147,
        157
    water power and, 150
    wind power and, 153–154

energy
    geothermal energy, 151–153, *152*, 157
    history of production of, 15–18
    independence in, 139–140
    for lighting, 15, 17–18, 27, 50
    natural gas and, 143–144
    nuclear energy, 147–150
    renewable energy, 144–147, 157
    solar energy, 4, 155–156, 157
    solutions to energy problems based on fossil
        fuels, 140–144, 158
    wind power, 15, *16*, 153–154, *153*, 157

environment
    acid rain and, 136–138
    blowout prevention and, 36
    coal and, 135–136, 140
    Deepwater Horizon disaster and, 127,
        128–131
    fossil fuels and, 127, 134, 136, 138
    global warming and, 134–135, 167
    greenhouse gases and, 133–134, 136, 143
    hydrocarbons and, 131–138
    oil industry and, 25–26, 127–128
    oil sands and, 142–143
    seeps and, 127–128, 129

wind power and, 154

Environmental Protection Agency, 138

ethanol
    as biofuel, 144–146
    production plant, *145*

Europe. *See also* Belgium; France; Germany;
        Great Britain; World War I; World
        War II
    automobiles and, 51, 52, 53, 56
    coal use and, 16–17, 92
    horses as transportation in, 54
    Islamic attitudes toward, 43
    Middle Eastern oil and, 56, 68
    trade and, 39

European Jews, 95–96

Exxon, 30, 98

ExxonMobil, 31

Exxon Valdez spill, 120–121, *120, 121,* 127, 129,
        130, 140, 142

F

Faisal I (king of Iraq), 60–61, 108

Faisal III (king of Iraq), 108

Faisal Ibn Abdul Aziz (king of Saudi Arabia),
        99–100

fertilizers, 93, 124, 137, 145, 157

Finnegan, Sean, 50

firepots, 14

food production, green revolution in, 93

Ford, Henry
    assembly-line production of automobiles
        and, 52–53, *53*
    photograph of, *52*

Ford Model T, 53

fossil fuels. *See also* coal; natural gas; oil
    defined, 167
    energy independence and, 139–140
    environmental effects of, 127, 134, 136, 138
    formation of, 5–10
    historical use of, 12
    as nonrenewable resource, 122, 158
    shortages of, 123–124
    solutions to energy problems based on,
        140–144

fossils
    Alethopteris serii, 4
    forms of, 4–5
    in La Brea Tar Pits, 12

179

Y

Z